FAMILY INC.

FAMILY INC.

Using Business Principles to Maximize
Your Family's Wealth

Douglas P. McCormick

WILEY

For general information on our other products and services or for technical support, please contact our Customer Care Department within the United States at (800) 762-2974, outside the United States at (317) 572-3993, or fax (317) 572-4002.

Wiley publishes in a variety of print and electronic formats and by print-on-demand. Some material included with standard print versions of this book may not be included in e-books or in print-on-demand. If this book refers to media such as a CD or DVD that is not included in the version you purchased, you may download this material at http://booksupport.wiley.com. For more information about Wiley products, visit www.wiley.com.

ISBN 978-1-119-21973-6 (Hardcover)
ISBN 978-1-119-21976-7 (ePDF)
ISBN 978-1-119-21974-3 (ePub)

Printed in the United States of America.
10 9 8 7 6 5 4 3 2 1

CONTENTS

I have watched Doug McCormick employ the lessons and teachings of *Family Inc.* for over 25 years. We became good friends as cadets at the United States Military Academy, where we endured the "Academy experience"— the rigors of school, military training, and the challenges of collegiate athletics; Doug as an accomplished wrestler and captain of the team and me battling on the gridiron for the football team. During that time, he established himself as a leader, an intense competitor, and a gifted, creative intellect, known for independent thinking. These attributes have propelled Doug to success through every stage of life: highest-ranking cadet and First Captain of the Corps, accomplished Army officer, distinguished student at Harvard Business School, and successful banker, investor, and entrepreneur as co-founder of HCI Equity Partners.

The breadth of his experience allows him to bring a unique perspective to the topic of personal finance. As an unemployed husband and father putting himself through Harvard Business School, Doug learned the challenges of acquiring wealth when you have none. Harvard exposed him to the best teachers and thinkers in finance. At Morgan Stanley, he developed an understanding of capital raising, mergers and acquisitions, and how Wall Street works and thinks. As a private equity investor and cofounder of his own firm, Doug understands business, entrepreneurship, and the tools corporate America uses to create enduring value. Few professionals have enjoyed such consistent success combined with such breadth of experience. His diverse life experience, educational accomplishments, and business experience make him uniquely qualified to advise us all on the pursuit of financial independence.

Family Inc. is a career road map and investment guide for everyone, regardless of life stage, education level, or profession. It offers valuable tools that would have helped me navigate my own career and financial progression as a student, Army officer, banker at Goldman Sachs, and CFO of the

NFL and Twitter. In many cases, I was following Doug's recommendations intuitively, but without understanding how they fit into the Family Inc. paradigm. My experiences are not unique. The book's teachings are relevant to the many people I have worked with throughout my career—for the soldier transitioning to civilian life, the banker with significant financial knowledge, the professional athlete who acquires wealth early in life, the millennials in Silicon Valley pursuing entrepreneurship, and my college-age daughter. Quite simply, *Family Inc.* is required reading for the Noto family. If you are going to read ONE personal finance book, this should be it.

In a field where so much has been studied, written, and restudied, it is hard to believe that it is possible to offer new, fresh, and compelling advice. However, this is exactly what Doug accomplishes. Most financial planning advice emanates from the Wall Street–centric perspective of professional investors and advisers, financial institutions, and organizations attempting to address your financial needs through products. Doug's approach is rooted in the insight that with the exception of the size of the numbers, corporate and family financial statements and the principles required to effectively manage them are essentially the same. He borrows best practices of corporate America and modifies them to fit your personal financial situation. This approach results in better decision making, which will lead to better outcomes and lower risk—and, I daresay, the purchase of fewer financial products.

Throughout the book, you will be exposed to numerous novel ways to think about the financial game of life Doug refers to as Family Inc. Examples of these conclusions include:

- For most of us, our labor represents our most significant asset. *Family Inc.* provides advice on how to most efficiently harvest this asset through investment and career choices. When is the last time you discussed your labor capital with your financial adviser?

- Any accurate measure of wealth or asset allocation must include your expected labor and Social Security values. This changes everything and is unheard of on Wall Street!

- Most investment programs are designed to minimize price volatility over relatively short planning horizons. *Family Inc.* recommends a portfolio that maximizes long-term, real, after-tax purchasing power in spite of shorter-term volatility. This results in significantly higher equity exposure than traditional advice has.

- Buy a home, enjoy it, and use it to create wonderful memories, but don't justify the purchase as a good investment.

- Labor and capital are commodities. Through entrepreneurship, you can help shelter these assets from competition.

- Mastering the lessons in the book can also help you maximize the impact of your charitable giving.

- Every family needs someone—the Family CFO—to ensure the members adequately manage their risks while effectively allocating both labor and financial capital to achieve financial independence.

Family Inc. was written as a user's guide for the individual. I am confident reading it will improve your financial wellbeing. But I would be remiss if I did not mention Doug's motive for writing the book and the public policy implications of this kind of fresh thinking in America today. Our economy and society are changing in ways that are making financial literacy more important than ever before, yet the disparities between those who have mastered these skills and those who have not continue to increase. While our political parties become more extreme in their approaches to address these symptoms, there is inadequate focus on educating Americans with the skills and tools to adapt to these changes and close this disparity. The kind of holistic, unbiased, actionable advice offered in this book must not only find its way into our formal education system but also into the family dialog. Regardless of your education, profession, wealth, or age, *Family Inc.* is meant for you.

Family Inc. is a great personal finance book. More important, it is a guide to personal empowerment.

Anthony Noto
CFO, Twitter Inc.

ACKNOWLEDGMENTS

To my son, Mike, and my daughter, Kelly, this book is my gift to you as you embark on the management of our family businesses. You are both already on the path of financial independence. Because of the investments you have made in yourselves through your education, your journey is already well under way. It is my hope that these lessons serve you throughout your lives as you use these principles to make your own way in this world. Like a carpenter, mason, or metal craftsman sharing his trade with his children, I share these skills and lessons of my trade as an investor. Use these lessons in good health and ensure that your children someday inherit not only your assets, but also these lessons so that they may be good stewards of our family business as well.

Mom, thanks for your unwavering confidence and support. Dad, thanks for getting me started in this crazy business with my first stock purchase at the ripe old age of seven. And thanks to Dave, my brother, role model, and adviser with sound judgment and pure intent.

To the Crown Fellow Program and my classmates, thanks for demanding significance.

To my partners and colleagues at HCI Equity, past and present, thanks for teaching me the business and putting up with me.

To my editor, Bill Rukeyser, thanks for helping me find a voice for this important subject matter that is straightforward, accessible, and even occasionally entertaining, without compromising the intellectual integrity of the recommendations.

To my wife, Michele, thanks for being my partner in life and our Family Business!

Additional Praise for
Family Inc.

"Stated succinctly, *Family Inc.* is one of the best books on family/personal finance I have read—and I have read many. McCormick's unique approach to labor and asset accumulation sets the foundation for an enjoyable and relevant read from start to finish, and the personal examples keep it real and engaging."

> —James Schenck, CEO, Pentagon Federal Credit Union

"*Family Inc.* is not a 'how to' book—it is a 'how to think' book that empowers the reader to take control of their family's finances. McCormick presents sophisticated financial principles and concepts in an accessible way, and teaches the reader how to tailor and apply them to their situation to achieve their financial and life goals. If you want one good book to read, reread, and keep as a long-term financial reference, *Family Inc.* is the book for you."

> —Brigadier General Mike Meese, USA retired and COO, American Armed Forces Mutual Aid Association

"Mission accomplished! This easy-to-read masterpiece provides a well-organized framework and process to review personal/family finances. Doug uses the disciplined approach of a successful business to explain key financial and life goal concepts, which will allow you and your family to confidently chart your own course to financial independence."

> —Herman Bulls, Vice Chairman, Americas JLL, Director, USAA, and former Assistant Professor of Economics at The United States Military Academy at West Point

"Financial planning in an uncertain world is hard; the unique sacrifices of our service members and veterans make this even harder. However, *Family Inc.* gives you tools to effectively evaluate and develop your financial 'self-worth' and, in turn, improve your financial security. It's a must have for your life skills 'tool kit.'"

> —Cutler Dawson, President and CEO, Navy Federal Credit Union

WITH APPRECIATION FOR AMERICA'S ARMED FORCES SERVICE MEMBERS

Most of us are aware of and can appreciate the sacrifices our country's service members have made to ensure our safety and freedom since 9/11/2001. They endure hardship and extended time away from loved ones, frequently putting themselves in harm's way for our collective benefit. However, there is much less appreciation of the financial sacrifices and hardships many service members endure long after their service. In many cases, they are required to move numerous times during their service, making it difficult for other family members to maximize their professional opportunities. Their active duty experiences are often underappreciated in other professional fields when service members attempt to transition from the military, and they experience higher rates of disability, divorce, and homelessness than the general population. All these factors threaten the financial security and welfare of our veterans.

Financial literacy can't eliminate these challenges, but it can mitigate their impact. I hope this book can serve as a valuable tool for veteran service organizations that are helping veterans while promoting awareness of the unique financial challenges our service members face. If you have suggestions or ideas about how this book can assist veterans in your community or organization, contact veteransupport@familyinc.com.

A quick Internet stroll down the Amazon search aisle for Personal Finance and Investment yields a long list of popular book titles—*Rich Dad, Poor Dad: What the Rich Teach Their Kids About Money*; *Total Money Makeover*; and Jim Cramer's *Getting Back to Even*, to name a few. While I have found some of these books enjoyable reading, most of the current universe of financial planning literature disappoints. Oversimplified "how-to" books of financial goal setting or technical works focused on a specific financial activity or asset class are not conducive to effective overall financial planning.

The principles upon which *Family Inc.* has been developed are based on proven corporate finance concepts modified to address personal financial planning and therefore are both timeless and time tested. This book is written, I hope, with the intellectual rigor of a corporate finance class but in the language of family discussion, with many examples from my own family.

Family Inc. is intended for people who have the potential to become high-income earners and want to develop a comprehensive, actionable, customized plan, one that acknowledges the relationships between job, net worth, age, consumption pattern, and long-term financial objectives. While it cannot guarantee financial security, it will give you the tools to develop a comprehensive financial plan and fully appreciate the implications of your decisions.

As a professional investor, I have spent substantial time analyzing various businesses and evaluating the financial profile of good companies. I have become involved in all financial aspects of the businesses my company invests in—strategic planning, financial analysis, budgeting, capital structure, capital raising, acquisitions, and restructurings. During the past 15 years, I have served all these businesses as an active board member or chairman of the board and in some cases as chief financial officer.

I realized along the way that many of the financial principles employed by successful companies are also relevant to personal financial planning and management. In these pages, I share those principles and recommendations for creating your own financial prosperity and security. The lessons are particularly timely in the current economic climate. While it may be comforting in these uncertain times to rely on a financial "expert" to manage your financial interests, only you can adequately prepare your family for the financial opportunities and challenges that lie ahead. Many people allow their financial adviser to manage them. This book will teach you how to manage your adviser—he or she does, after all, work for you.

One last point before we begin our journey. These principles and concepts of financial planning assume that you have the discipline and intellectual honesty to act rationally and stick to your financial plan. For example, many advisers suggest that you pay off the mortgage on your primary residence as quickly as possible. On the contrary, I recommend that you pay off real estate debt last (even after making other investments), given the relatively low after-tax cost of this debt. But this assumes that you actually save and reinvest this increased cash flow and don't blow it on a new flat screen or vacation. For these principles to work for you, you need to know yourself and your family members and customize these lessons appropriately for your personal situation.

Now let's begin the journey of developing your comprehensive road map to financial security and independence.

EVERY FAMILY NEEDS A CHIEF FINANCIAL OFFICER

CHAPTER 1

Why Do I Need a CFO? I Don't Even Own a Business

Growing up, my brother, Dave, and I developed different attitudes and behavior about money. Dave's nickname was Spendsworth, given to him by our grandfather because, as Grandpa said, "He spends what he is worth." Dave supported his carefree spending because he always seemed to have some sort of job. Making money wasn't the hard part for him; holding on to it seemed to be. Like any good younger brother, I took the opposite tack. I, too, had many jobs—newspaper deliverer, farmhand, babysitter, Christmas tree trimmer, and stationery salesman, to name a few. But I saved almost everything I earned, made some investments with my father's help and even loaned some of it out to poor Spendsworth at usurious interest rates.

While most of these youthful habits have stood me in good stead, they haven't exempted me from the sometimes scary financial decisions and challenges that come with becoming an adult. In my twenties, I resigned an Army commission to go to Harvard Business School just as my wife, Michele, became pregnant with our first child. While the opportunity to attend Harvard was exciting, it came at a high cost. Boston was much more expensive than we anticipated, and the job Michele got at Harvard barely covered child care and housing. Because I had some modest savings, I wasn't eligible for financial aid. For the next two years, we depleted my savings and borrowed heavily to pay for school, fund living expenses, and carry a monthly mortgage on our previous house, which we ultimately sold for a $50,000 loss. As my savings dwindled, so did much of my confidence, replaced by the humility and sense of helplessness that many families experience in the face of financial hardship.

Even when I was a newly minted MBA, the financial losses continued. We had to borrow money from a family friend to move to New York, where we spent our first night sleeping on the floor, sweating with no air conditioning in the city's summer heat. Lying there, feeling more than a little defeated, I realized that in spite of a lot of effort and hard work, bad financial decision making had put us in this precarious situation. I was still managing our finances as I had as a young single man. It would take another decade of more learning and more mistakes to make sense of how my everyday life decisions fit together financially into the precepts for success on which this book is based.

Many of us go to great pains to separate our work life from our family life, and to leave "business" out of the family equation. But doing so diminishes our ability to make sound decisions about our financial future—and the financial future of each of our family members. What I'll introduce in this chapter, and elaborate on in the chapters that follow, is how to apply the business principles of corporate finance to your own personal wealth management decisions.

Asset and liability management, practical financial statements, control of risks, asset allocation, tax planning—all are tools in the world of corporate finance that help companies achieve their goals. And there's no reason these techniques can't be adopted for your personal use. Every business has a CFO—a chief financial officer—and every family needs one.

Though few people think about it this way, everybody owns not just one but two distinct businesses: a temporary labor business and an asset management business, which together comprise Family Inc.

1. Your temporary labor business. Each of us is born with a finite amount of labor potential to be harvested over a lifetime. Regardless of whether you are an employee in a large company, a soldier in the Army, or a small business owner, in all cases you are in the same

basic business converting your labor into money. Like natural resources such as coal, natural gas, or gold, your labor potential is finite and is depleted over time. As part of a family, it's not just your own labor you need to consider, but that of your family members as well. The financial objective of your temporary labor business is to convert your labor into financial assets as efficiently as possible. In any job, your temporary labor business sells your skills and energy.

2. **Your asset management business.** The second business is an asset management business that manages the assets you have acquired through your temporary labor business or by other means, such as inheritance. These assets might include your home, your savings, your 401(k), and more. Your objective in your asset management business is twofold: (1) manage and enlarge your portfolio of assets; and (2) produce adequate cash flow to support both your consumption needs—everything from groceries, clothes, and car expenses to recreation—and investments to further your labor business, such as my return to graduate school for further education that enhanced my earning power.

These businesses are complementary and interdependent, and they must be managed in a coordinated manner. Your objectives as CFO in managing these two businesses can be simplified into three basic goals:

1. Provide adequate cash flow to support your spending, now and in the future, while allowing necessary investments to enhance those two businesses of yours: labor and asset management.

2. Maximize your "Family Inc. Net Worth"—the sum of your labor and financial assets after taxes.

3. Manage your legacy by maximizing what you can leave to family members (and their ability to manage these assets) or to worthy causes. While this goal is worthwhile, it is a distant third in priority. You can't do number 3 without first accomplishing both 1 and 2.

To illustrate the interaction between these businesses over time, let's take a simplified snapshot of one young man's current financial situation, encompassing all the assets he has to work with, which include estimates of future compensation for his work, future returns on his investments, and future

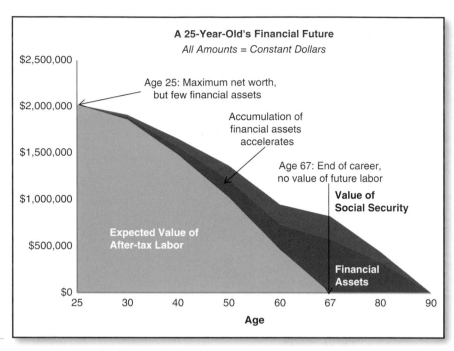

FIGURE 1.1 The Three Parts of Family Inc. Net Worth and How They Evolve Over Time

Social Security payments, based on assumptions that are reasonable today.* Throughout this book we present examples like this one that illustrate key concepts by representing common circumstances. Tools to personalize the examples to fit you and your family can be found at familyinc.com.

These assumptions allow us to generate the holistic view in Figure 1.1 of the young man's projected Family Inc. Net Worth over his lifetime, including the value in today's money (that is, 2016 dollars) of the expected future assets generated by both of his businesses after all of his spending. For example, Figure 1.1 shows that at age 25 he estimates his *expected lifetime labor value* (compensation for his work,

*The assumptions: He is 25, has no financial assets—or liabilities—and a starting job that pays $44,500 per year, the average salary for college graduates in 2013. We assume he will work for 42 years. As his skills develop, he expects his salary will grow at 2.0 percent annually in *real* terms (adjusted for inflation) through his retirement at 67. His annual contributions to taxes, Social Security, and other required deductions approximate 30 percent of his gross salary. He saves and invests 10 percent of his after-tax salary throughout his career and estimates his investments will provide an annual return of 5.0 percent after inflation, fees, and taxes. Today's Social Security eligibility rules apply with an assumed benefit equal to the average 2014 benefit for a single-income earner. He plans to consume all his savings during retirement through level, inflation-adjusted annual consumption through age 90—the financial equivalent of a 23-year annuity.

shown in green) at about $2 million. (For details on how to calculate expected lifetime labor value, see the Appendix.) By age 40, as the chart indicates, he will have received almost $500,000 of that value, so his remaining labor value has shrunk to $1.5 million. However, that $500,000 of used-up labor has funded his living expenses for the past 15 years while also allowing him to accumulate over $75,000 in savings and other financial assets (shown in red). By age 40 he has also paid enough into Social Security to earn some $95,000 in expected future Social Security payments (shown in purple). By age 67, he will have retired, so he'll have no remaining earnings—he depleted the $1.5 million of potential earnings over the 27 years since he was 40—but his financial assets have increased to about $570,000 and his expected Social Security payments to more than $250,000. At 67, he will have to use these assets to support his spending for the rest of his life.

As Figure 1.1 demonstrates, Family Inc. Net Worth embodies three key components: (1) the value in today's money of expected after-tax labor income; (2) the value in today's money of after-tax future Social Security benefits; and (3) net financial assets (financial assets minus financial liabilities). In summary, the family converts labor into money and future Social Security payments during working years so it can use these assets to fund consumption during retirement.

This graphic is oversimplified, and the assumptions, based on today's realities, are certain to be off base because circumstances will change. Yet the concepts, insights, and planning tools that it facilitates remain powerful. First and foremost, this 25-year-old has an estimate of what his future financial life might look like if he doesn't go back to school. If, however, he were thinking of leaving his job to go to law school, he could modify these assumptions to reflect the impact of becoming a lawyer and compare the two scenarios. Figure 1.1 highlights several concepts that we will explore in greater depth throughout the book.

Family Inc. Net Worth is an expanded definition of net worth (all your financial assets minus all your liabilities) that includes as assets the value today of anticipated lifetime after-tax income and Social Security benefits. Including these as assets highlights several critical principles:

- For most people, future earnings from work are the largest asset, so the greatest net worth is achieved at a time when financial assets are minimal. This dramatizes the *opportunity cost* (the value you give up to get something else) of wasted labor, unemployment, or "excess" schooling, as well as the negative implications of failing to save or invest some of your wages. It shows that if our 25-year-old does pursue a law degree, to make this a good *financial* decision he'd better earn enough more in his new job to compensate him for his school costs and his lost earnings while studying.

- In the later years of your Family Inc., success is driven by the power of increased earnings and compounding financial assets. Figure 1.1 shows it takes this man about 25 years to accumulate $180,000 of financial assets, but in the next 17 years, those assets more than triple to about $570,000. For your financial assets to benefit from this exponential growth, you must start the saving and compounding process early. Delaying savings until later in adulthood puts you at a substantial disadvantage in the quest for financial security.

- Money management skills are a critical and often overlooked precondition for financial security. As Figure 1.1 suggests, savings and capital appreciation represent approximately 20 percent of the total assets available for consumption over a lifetime (including labor and Social Security benefits), yet most people spend significantly less time on managing this part of their business. Do you know anyone who spends 20 percent of his or her professional efforts on personal asset management activities?

In the context of the Family Inc. Net Worth framework, Social Security should be viewed as nothing more than the mandatory purchase of an inflation-indexed annuity that is guaranteed by the government—just another part of your financial asset portfolio.* By itself, this asset will not provide financial security, and future changes in policy are likely to decrease these benefits. Regardless, for most people, Social Security benefits are an attractive asset and an important part of a financial planning program.

While our labor assets are by definition finite—we all die sometime—*capital assets* (investments) can grow without limit and, if managed correctly, can provide a perpetual annuity whose annual gains and income exceed consumption. This is the ultimate accomplishment in achieving financial security because it means you've practically eliminated the risk of outliving your assets.

■ Assumptions and Reality

Employing this Family Inc. Net Worth framework allows an individual or family to identify the 10 key variables that ultimately influence their financial security. These variables include:

1. Labor wage rates: Salary and bonuses.

2. Labor duration: How long can you work?

---

*An annuity provides a stream of fixed payments over a specified period; an inflation-indexed annuity adjusts payments over time to reflect inflation and preserve purchasing power.

3. Savings rates: How much of your after-tax income will you save?

4. Consumption profile: How much will you spend?

5. Reinvestment rates: What return can you expect on your money after fees and taxes?

6. Life expectancy.

7. Family inheritance.

8. Tax rates on income, capital gains, and estates.

9. Social Security eligibility and policy.

10. Inflation rates.

While we'll explore the potential impact of all these variables in greater detail throughout this book, note that you can influence items 1 through 7. With the benefit of more information, they can be adjusted over time to help you achieve your financial goals. You have no influence over items 8 through 10, but they also have a significant impact on all business owners and must be considered in your financial planning.

The same assumptions used to develop the Family Inc. Net Worth forecasts in Figure 1.1 can also be translated into a Family Inc. Cash Flow Projection. A Family Inc. Cash Flow Projection represents cash that will be available throughout life to cover living expenses *after* your taxes, planned savings, and debt repayments (if you have any).

Figure 1.2 projects the dollars available, adjusted for inflation, over our 25-year-old's future years of consumption. In the early years, his consump-

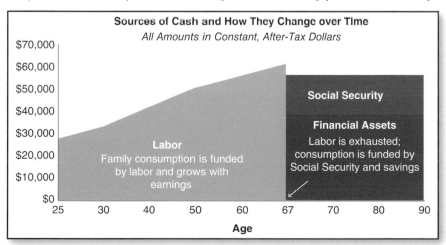

FIGURE 1.2   Annual Family Inc. Cash Flow Projection

tion is funded by his largest asset—labor. As he gets older and his labor is depleted, he has to fund consumption from his financial assets. Figure 1.2 also highlights some of the challenges of managing your businesses in a way that satisfies your family's needs. It's useful because it suggests a spending pattern a person could adopt over time while incurring no debt and saving 10 percent of after-tax earnings, but it's theoretical. In reality, no one's cash flow looks just like this. For example, this Family Spending Profile is often inconsistent with the financial needs of a young family—including mine. At 28, I stopped working and returned to school to pursue an MBA. For two years, my wife, child, and I spent approximately $50,000 annually more than we earned after tax. We maintained consumption that was much higher than our earnings by depleting our limited savings and borrowing money. Later on, to meet my savings goal, we had to consume dramatically less than we earned for several years to make up for this deficit.

Even though my financial assets decreased dramatically, the principles of this book demonstrate that the effect on our Family Inc. Net Worth was positive almost from day one. During my two years in graduate school, our financial assets plummeted to about negative $100,000: I depleted my financial assets to zero and also borrowed $100,000 in school loans to make this major investment in my labor development. However, at the same time, thanks to the value of the degree and the skills and relationships I developed, the expected value of my labor went up dramatically to more than offset the depletion of financial assets. In other words, between ages 28 and 30, my Family Inc. Net Worth increased in aggregate: Financial assets decreased but the increase in labor assets more than made up for that loss.

Families often have greater consumption needs early in their life cycle when they have children and make significant purchases like housing, education, furniture, and automobiles. A Family CFO might choose to use debt to finance major investments such as a house purchase, or change savings rates over time. While these actions make more capital available in the short term, they do so at the expense of future consumption and introduce additional risk into the long-term financial security of the family, so they must be done prudently.

The real world offers other challenges to the theoretical Family Inc. Cash Flow Projection. The amount of spending that can be supported by interest, dividends, and capital gains from investments is sensitive to assumptions about how long family members will live and how investments will perform, both of which are unpredictable and subject to sudden changes. Finally, this profile assumes that retirement and Social Security both start at

67 and that full Social Security benefits are received. Both of these assumptions are uncertain.

Given the uncertainty, a financial plan must include a reasonable cushion against the risk of financial distress or shortfall. The adage that you can't take it with you is absolutely correct, but so is the unfortunate reality that it is all too easy to outlive your assets and become a financial burden on your family.

Many people believe that if they can't accurately predict their financial future, a plan is of little use. In my business, we often joke that there are two types of financial plans: lucky and lousy. I expect *every* financial plan to be wrong. The value in the plan is the discipline of explicitly defining your assumptions and alerting you to changes in these assumptions. A sound financial plan must be dynamic, evolving, and subject to frequent scrutiny with the benefit of additional information. Fortunately, several of the key drivers of Family Inc. Net Worth, such as retirement age, savings rates, and consumption levels, can be modified as needed to address failures in your estimates or your changing circumstances. You have some control over when you decide to retire and how much you spend and save.

■ But What Does a Family Chief Financial Officer Specifically Do?

We have established the key concept that every family actually owns two distinct businesses, both of which must be actively managed. But we still haven't addressed the specific responsibilities of the Family CFO. While the following list is not all-inclusive, it provides a sense of the responsibilities of the position and some of the topics we cover in the following pages.

Cash management—making sure the family has adequate funds to satisfy short-term cash needs such as monthly expenses, bills, loan payments, and unexpected contingencies.

Balance sheet management—managing the composition of the family's assets and liabilities to balance competing needs for liquidity, tolerable risk, and appreciation.

Income statement management—managing the family's incoming cash, such as salaries, and outgoing cash, such as monthly expenses. This includes developing the family budget and monitoring how actual results compare to the budget.

Family labor decisions and development—managing and investing in labor skills to ensure access to the best employment opportunities.

Risk management—managing risk through effective self or third-party insurance programs.

Asset allocation and investment decisions—developing an asset allocation and investment program customized for your Family Business's needs and your willingness to accept risks.

Managing investments in entrepreneurship—funding family owned businesses to complement your human and financial resources.

Adviser management—managing a variety of specialists such as financial advisers, lawyers, and estate planners to support your financial planning needs.

Tax and estate planning—developing and managing a tax and estate program to minimize liabilities.

Education—teaching your family the lessons and skills of a Family CFO.

Succession planning—creating an environment that allows your heirs to develop as CFOs to perpetuate your family legacy.

These extensive responsibilities of the Family CFO are critical to the financial well-being of the family.

■ The Big Picture

Long-term trends within the United States and around the world have dramatically increased the need for every family to have a member with the skills and knowledge to adequately manage the family's business interests and financial affairs—a Family CFO. Some influential trends include:

People are living longer. In 1960, the average time between retirement and death for men in America was approximately four years (retired at age 66, deceased by 70). Today, that interval has widened to approximately 16 years. Because of this 300 percent increase, many workers will be required to support themselves with their accumulated financial assets long after they retire.

People change jobs more often. An increasingly global economy and the resulting competition have resulted in a more dynamic business environment with more rapid change and uncertainty for both employees and companies. Today's young professional is likely to hold more than 10 different jobs over the course of a career. This vigorous job mobility—both voluntary and involuntary—significantly reduces the likelihood of a long-term relationship between an individual and a single employer. The days of a paternalistic employer and lifetime employment are gone.

Fewer people belong to unions, participate in collective bargaining agreements, or have defined-benefit retirement plans. Over the past 35 years, the percentage of Americans who belong to a union or participate in a collective bargaining agreement has decreased by approximately half. Over a similar period, the number of private and governmental defined-benefit pension plans (the traditional plans that promise to pay retirees a set annual amount) has also shrunk by half—and by two-thirds in the private sector. In their place, 401(k)s and other defined-contribution plans, in which the individual is responsible for investment decisions, have about quadrupled. These trends, part of corporate America's attempt to remain globally competitive, have shifted risk from employers to individuals.

The costs of health care and education have ballooned. Access to education and health care is critical to successfully managing Family Inc. However, individuals have little control over these costs, which continue to increase at alarming rates. Long-term inflation in the United States has averaged about 3.4 percent per year. Health care and education costs have increased two to three times as fast.

Funding for traditional government entitlement programs is uncertain. Rising costs for safety net programs such as Medicare, Medicaid, and Social Security, accelerated by changes in demographics that are increasing the number of recipients, are contributing to the overall federal and state deficits. Clearly, these trends are unsustainable, so changes to these programs are likely. Families must prepare for negative shocks.

The financial landscape is getting more and more complex. Half a century of deregulation combined with product innovation and proliferation has multiplied the complexity of financial choices in the areas of credit, investment, and insurance, increasing the need for financial literacy and independence. Examples include:

■ Consumer credit. The first plastic charge card with broad retail acceptance was issued in 1958 by American Express. U.S.

consumers today possess some 610 million credit cards, representing almost 3.5 credit cards per cardholder.

- Investment choices. The Securities and Exchange Act of 1936 and the Investment Company Act of 1940 helped democratize the financial markets, allowing the retail investment market to flourish. In 1970, there were approximately 360 mutual funds with $48 billion in assets. According to the Investment Company Institute, approximately 7,600 U.S. mutual funds hold $12 trillion in assets today.

- Insurance products. While the concept of risk sharing or pooling through insurance has been around for centuries, these products have also undergone substantial innovation and growth, with global insurance premiums reaching approximately $4.6 trillion in 2012. The United States accounts for more than 25 percent of global premiums, while representing less than 5 percent of global population. Today's consumer has more than 150 distinct types of insurance to choose from.

These trends have changed the nature of the game. Your grandfather likely worked for one or two companies during his career, and the family's wealth was primarily a product of his cumulative compensation and retirement benefits. The future for today's generation looks very different. The social contract between the employee and the employer will continue to evolve in ways that ensure that companies maintain flexibility to remain globally competitive: mergers, downsizing, eliminating poorly performing employees, and replacing labor with technology. At the same time, employees will benefit from increasing freedom to move among opportunities that offer the best personal development, career progress, and compensation. Employment has become a game of free agency.

While this evolution is scary to some, it's the reality of a global marketplace. For those who embrace this change and systematically develop valuable, enduring professional skills—those who are capable of performing the role of Family CFO and effectively managing Family Inc.—these trends create increased opportunity for financial success and security. Employing the concepts conveyed in this book will provide you with the skills and foundation of knowledge to effectively develop and manage your family's financial well-being amid real world challenges and choices.

■ Key Conclusions

You are a business owner. Each of us owns two businesses—a temporary labor business and an asset management business. This insight allows the Family CFO to use many of the everyday tools of the world of business to navigate important family decisions such as career choice, retirement, and education.

Most financial plans (and planners) ignore your biggest assets, especially labor. Including these assets in your Family Inc. Net Worth will dramatically change your conclusions.

Your role as the Family CFO is much broader than balancing the checkbook. Your important responsibilities include assisting in career and education decisions, budgeting, investing, managing risk, and retirement planning.

The changes in the world around you are making these skills increasingly necessary.

MAXIMIZE THE VALUE OF YOUR SINGLE BIGGEST ASSET—YOUR LABOR

In Section I, we concluded that the value of the family's future labor represents a majority of the family assets for most families. So an important role of the Family CFO is to ensure that this asset value is maximized. People often base career choices—labor allocation decisions in this context—on many different factors such as values, job satisfaction, compensation, and quality of life. Section II focuses on only one of these criteria—lifetime compensation. That is not to say that you should make your career choice based on that criterion alone, but rather overlay your own priorities on the financial considerations presented here.

CHAPTER 2

Double the Value of Your Labor through Education

Perhaps because my father was an educator, he set some pretty crazy academic expectations for my brother and me. Early on, he conveyed the concept that every academic accomplishment is a building block for future success—success in middle school sets you up for high school, high school for college, and college for life. So went the logic. He actually had me convinced when I was a fifth-grader that colleges would consider my elementary school transcript.

Dad never had the formal education in finance that I have. But when I look at the lessons he taught my brother and me about the importance of education, and the choices he made for his own education, it's clear he understood that the surest path to wealth creation is investing in yourself to develop valuable skills through education.

Dad completed his undergraduate degree in two and a half years and was a practicing teacher by the age of 19. After several years of teaching, he completed his master's degree and earned a principal's certificate by age 25. After several years in this managerial role, Dad returned to school to complete his doctoral degree, which allowed him to make the jump to college dean. He continued to invest in developing his skills throughout his career, attending a Harvard executive education program, pursuing studies during his sabbatical, and investing time in professional organizations that offered the opportunity to network and learn from his peers. Let's be clear: My father didn't become a teacher to make lots of money—no one does. However, his educational choices did allow him to maximize his career potential, which often also maximizes your financial potential in your selected career.

Several themes in Dad's educational choices apply to any career:

> *Pursuing education early in your career pays the biggest dividends.* Dad was benefiting from his first educational investment by the time he was 19 and had many years to reap the rewards.

> *Education is most valuable when complemented by relevant experience.* Early in his career, Dad left and returned to the work force three times, each time bringing new skills and experience. Knowledge must be complemented by real world context and experience to maximize its impact.

> *Education doesn't stop in college.* Dad made it a point to ensure that he continued to invest in his career development long after he graduated from college. Just as a machine or your car can get dated and need upgrading or replacement, so will the skills you learned long ago in college.

> *Education and investment in your career should be both formal and informal.* You don't have to be in a classroom to be investing in your professional capabilities. Industry associations, networking events, even reading a book like this all count as investments in yourself and, ultimately, in Family Inc.

■ Educated People Earn More

The common perception among Americans is that higher levels of education offer better, higher paying professional opportunities, and this is generally true. Table 2.1 confirms the notion that the higher the education level, the more employable a person is. Median income tends to rise—and unemployment falls—by education level.* While this general correlation between

---

*Doctorates are an exception, at least regarding incomes. Median income for people with PhDs is about the same or somewhat lower than for those with professional degrees, probably because many PhDs choose lower-paying careers in academia.

education and compensation is intuitive to most, the magnitude of the economic benefit is often underestimated by not considering the impact over a full career. Incorporated into our Family Inc. Net Worth paradigm, the data show that more education is a compelling investment under most circumstances.

Figure 2.1 shows how each additional level of education raises annual and lifetime income (anticipated after-tax labor value) based on the following assumptions: expected *value of lifetime labor* for each level of education equals the present value of the after-tax median salary (*implied annual earnings* adjusted for median periods of unemployment for each education level) multiplied by the number of available years of work through age 67. Those reaching each education level begin working between the ages of 18 and 26, depending on education level attained, and remain employed through age 67. Assumed deductions for items such as taxes and Social Security for each education level range from 10 percent to 30 percent. The costs of education shown are typical, but variations in these costs are massive.

In Table 2.1, the first column shows how dramatically median pay rises with each additional level of education—and by implication, how lifetime earnings follow suit, since pay can be expected to increase over time. The second column displays the *present value* of a total lifetime of labor at each level. (Present value, a concept that will recur often in this book, is a future amount of money that has been discounted to reflect its current value, as if it existed today. A dollar today is worth more than a dollar tomorrow because money can earn interest and inflation erodes

TABLE 2.1	Education Pays Off			
Education Level	Implied Annual Earnings	Value of Lifetime Labor	Expected Cost of Education	Cumulative Gain vs. No Diploma
Doctoral	$82,539	$2,426,655	$120,000	$1,323,668
Professional	$87,078	$2,621,049	$100,000	$1,538,062
Master's	$66,758	$2,129,591	$75,000	$1,071,603
Bachelor's	$55,311	$1,971,850	$50,000	$938,863
Associate	$38,222	$1,526,976	$40,000	$503,989
Some college	$35,158	$1,518,814	$25,000	$510,826
High school graduate	$31,313	$1,409,090	$0	$426,102
No high school diploma	$21,844	$982,987	$0	$0

Source: Implied annual earnings: Bureau of Labor Statistics for 2013 (bls.gov).

the future purchasing power.) The third column estimates the tuition and other costs of each additional education level. Finally, in the fourth column, we see the incremental lifetime value of each level over the $982,987 a person without a high school diploma might expect to earn over a lifetime.

Assuming you achieve median compensation levels, investing $100,000 in higher education to receive a professional degree such as a law degree or MBA results in a gain of more than $1.5 million in the present value of your after-tax lifetime labor. That represents a 15.4-fold return on investment, or a real internal rate of return (IRR, the effective yield or interest rate on the investment) of approximately 12 percent a year. While we haven't yet covered principles of anticipated investment return, 12 percent a year is a very attractive return. Furthermore, this analysis likely underestimates the return on this investment. It doesn't account for additional forms of compensation such as stock ownership and options. Such forms of compensation are skewed toward more highly educated employees and often represent a significant portion of total income. This analysis also doesn't take into account that Social Security benefits are earned on the basis of income levels, so higher incomes will translate into higher Social Security benefits as well.

Income disparities related to education levels in the United States are likely to persist and keep growing for two primary reasons. First, the United States continues to migrate to a service-based economy that rewards intellectual capabilities over manual labor. The demand for jobs requiring education is likely to grow faster than for those that don't. Second, given the relatively high cost of labor in the United States, corporations that choose to maintain manufacturing capabilities here will likely do so through efficiencies gained from technology and automation, further reducing demand for jobs requiring less education.

■ Educated People Work Longer

We've established that education dramatically increases the expected value of a person's labor. Almost as important, education also increases the projected *amount* of labor. The analysis summarized in Table 2.1 assumes that people at all education levels exhaust their labor potential at age 67. Let's hope that we are financially secure enough that we have the liberty to retire at 67. However, while it can be difficult for a manual laborer to continue to work after 67, many highly educated people can work productively well beyond age 70 should their financial condition require them to do so. Let's assume the young man profiled in Figure 1.1 gets his professional degree and decides to work through age 70. This results in a projected increase of $219,000 of after-tax labor between the ages of 67 and 70, which is slightly more than 10 percent of his total after-tax labor potential. Including the increased capacity for labor raises the return on his $100,000 educational investment to more than 18 times.

The implications of this investment in education dramatically change his financial security. Not only does the education expand both his expected compensation and his earning years, but it also shortens by three years the time between retirement and death while adding three years for investments to grow before retirement. Figures 2.1 and 2.2 compare the financial consequences of his working until 67 and spending his savings over 23 years versus working to 70 and spending his savings over 20 years.

The incremental three years of earnings results in an increase of Family Inc. Net Worth of approximately $220,000, which results in increased consumption from ages 70 through 90 of approximately $15,500 a year—an increase of almost 30 percent.

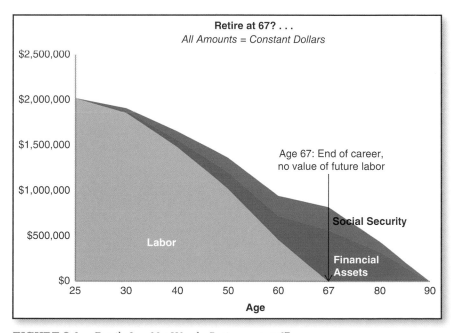

FIGURE 2.1 Family Inc. Net Worth–Retirement at 67

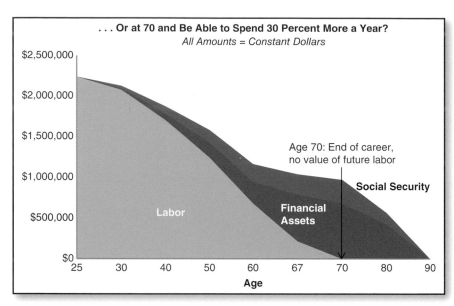

FIGURE 2.2   Family Inc. Net Worth–Retirement at 70

■ Not All Degrees Are Created Equal

These analyses are necessarily somewhat general in that they assume people pursue undergraduate education that is applicable to their business endeavors. There are great disparities even among college graduates, depending upon the type of skills, coursework, and employment. Table 2.2 ranks the undergraduate majors that generally lead to the best and worst paying jobs, from a sample ranking of 129 majors by median earnings after 15 years' experience. The conclusion is pretty straightforward: Quantitative and other skills that are commonly applied in a business environment garner compensation dramatically higher than "softer" skills focused on the humanities. The average of the top 10 mid-career salaries by undergraduate degree exceeds the bottom 10 by approximately $65,000 a year, or 137 percent. If you are making an investment in education, consider picking a degree that maximizes the value of this investment.

■ Education May Be a Great Investment, But How Do I Pay for It?

Many people will tell you that they wanted to pursue higher education but didn't feel they could afford it or weren't sure how they could pay for it. Given our investment analysis, it is clear that this is an investment you can't

TABLE 2.2	Majors Matter		
Rank	Undergraduate Degree	Median Starting Salary	Median Mid- Career Salary
1	Petroleum engineering	$103,000	$160,000
2	Actuarial mathematics	$58,700	$120,000
3	Nuclear engineering	$67,600	$117,000
4	Chemical engineering	$68,200	$115,000
5	Aerospace engineering	$62,800	$109,000
6	Electrical engineering	$64,300	$106,000
6 (tie)	Computer engineering	$65,300	$106,000
8	Computer science	$59,800	$102,000
9	Physics	$53,100	$101,000
10	Mechanical engineering	$60,900	$99,700
11–119			
120	Culinary arts	$34,800	$51,100
121	Exercise science	$32,600	$51,000
122	Horticulture	$35,200	$50,900
123	Biblical studies	$35,400	$50,800
124	Special education	$33,800	$49,600
125	Human development	$35,900	$48,000
126	Athletic training	$34,800	$46,900
127	Social work	$33,000	$46,600
128	Elementary education	$32,200	$45,300
129	Child and family studies	$30,300	$37,200

Source: 2013–2014 Pay Scale College Salary Report, www.payscale.com, March 15, 2014.

afford not to make. Fortunately, higher education institutions and the government offer numerous financing options that make the cost of borrowing low and the repayment schedule long.

Even if you have the cash to fund your schooling as you go, I recommend financing this expenditure and using your other capital to provide flexibility to make higher-return investments in the future. We explore this financing recommendation in Section III. For now, suffice it to say that education debt is relatively cheap because public policy often subsidizes the cost of these loans. They have a long repayment schedule (up to 25 years) and the interest is often tax deductible. These attributes make education loans attractive relative to most other types of financing.

Now that we have surveyed the financial implications of investments in education, let's revisit my father's experience to see how practice and theory compare. Dad started his first teaching job in 1961 with an annual salary of approximately $2,000 (about $16,000 in today's dollars). Over the next 10 years, he took time off for another two years of schooling that cost him approximately $6,000 in forgone after-tax income and tuition. However, this investment in education allowed him to assume greater responsibility, which resulted in peak earning years in excess of $350,000, compared to a high school teacher's estimated peak of about $90,000. Furthermore, Dad's education allowed him more flexibility in his retirement choices. The average retirement age of secondary school teachers is approximately 59. At 59, Dad had just assumed a new role as head of the Minnesota state system of higher education, which he performed for more than 10 years. Today, at 79, Dad is still at it. He is taking advantage of the decades-long investment that he has made in developing relationships across the education industry to serve as a recruiter for university leadership positions. Not only did Dad's investment in education allow him to earn more each year for his work, but it also gave him the skills to dramatically extend his productive work life. I estimate that Dad's investment choices in education (combined with his good performance) have so far allowed him to earn over $4 million more after taxes than he would have had he remained a high school teacher. Considering the $6,000 of forgone income, this seems like a pretty good investment. And the old boy is still going strong.

■ Reality Check

The cited payoffs from education assume that the student has the desire as well as the intellectual and personality attributes required to be successful. Back to my caution in the beginning of this book: People must be able to make an honest assessment of their capabilities and interests. While an education can be a valuable asset, this is only true if the student has the interest and aptitude to apply the education to his professional endeavors upon graduation. Financially, the worst outcome is for someone to make this investment, forgo the earnings opportunity while in school, and then not apply the education for financial benefit. If you don't intend to pursue a job that requires higher education, force yourself to acknowledge that before making the investment.

■ Key Conclusions

For people with the aptitude, skills, and personality to succeed in college, investments in education are one of the surest ways to financial security and wealth creation.

Most people already know that achieving a higher level of education translates into higher compensation, but there are numerous other, equally important benefits: less unemployment; more mobility to change jobs, locations, and industries; and the option to extend your career later in life.

The ability to extend a career is particularly important because it acts as a kind of insurance, allowing you to earn more if your financial goals haven't been achieved by your planned retirement age. Doing so dramatically increases your spending ability in your later years by not only raising your earning power, but also shrinking the number of years you expect to fund your spending exclusively from your financial assets.

Not all education offers the same economic benefit. As you contemplate investments in a career, consider that majors that develop math, science, and engineering skills generally offer the greatest economic reward.

CHAPTER 3

Make Career Choices that Extend Your Possibilities

DRS in canada have very little growth opportunity

People seeking career advice often ask what company or what job they should pursue. But if you correctly see yourself as a business owner managing your temporary labor business, these are the wrong questions. You should be asking instead what choices provide the most professional opportunity now and the most options for future growth. Today's workplace is too dynamic and your expected career is far too long to attempt to make good job choices based on future prospects for a specific company or position. Rather, choices should be made with the goal of maximizing the skills, relationships, and future options that can be thought of as constituting your personal brand—your perceived ability to compete effectively for increased responsibilities and compensation in a variety of roles, industries, and locations.

In general, people should pursue work experiences with the broadest range of applicability. Developing varied expertise in one or more business functions—finance, information technology, human resources, sales and marketing, or general management—allows an employee not only to change jobs, but also to change industries numerous times over a career. Since many of us may be working for half a century, the ability to choose between companies *and* industries to pursue the best opportunities and compensation is very valuable. Not having that flexibility can be costly. Consider the conundrum of airline pilots, general practice medical doctors, and others with labor skills that are relatively specific to a certain industry. These professions have undergone significant change over the past several decades, and as a result growth in compensation has underperformed the general labor markets. But because of their specialized skills, even talented employees in these fields are unlikely to change industries. Their plight highlights the benefits of acquiring functional expertise that can be redeployed to new industries with more attractive prospects.

■ Reconciling Contradictory Arguments

The advice in this chapter may seem to contradict the preceding chapter. There I highlighted the benefits of specialization, especially the rewards of higher levels of education and quantitative skills. Here I am promoting the benefits of being a generalist and the flexibility it offers to change organizations, positions, and industries. These recommendations are actually consistent. Specialized education with a bias toward the hard sciences and quantitative skills fosters one's problem-solving ability that can be applied broadly. To maximize the value of your lifetime labor, specialize with a bias toward hard skills in your education and seek varied professional roles and challenges in the workplace.

Ultimately, professionals who combine well-developed critical thinking and quantitative skills with broad generalist experiences can qualify for managerial roles and profit-and-loss responsibility (jobs that directly affect a company's bottom line). Because a general manager can have such a significant impact on the financial performance of a business, it's no coincidence that CEOs—essentially generalists and general managers—are so highly paid. Recent studies of S&P 500 companies show that their generalist leaders averaged approximately $10.5 million in annual compensation, which is more than 250 times the average employee's salary. If they do their job well, CEOs have skills that are highly fungible among different companies and industries and can result in significant value creation.

■ Allocate Your Labor Like a Growth Investor Allocates Capital

When I make investment decisions with my capital, I am a value investor because I must carefully balance the risk of loss versus the likelihood of gain. When I make career decisions, I invest my labor like a growth investor—emphasizing higher-reward opportunities in spite of the higher risks that go with them. The primary reason for this different approach to risk is that there is no risk of loss for your labor other than opportunity cost. If the risky venture doesn't work out, you simply take your labor, your recent experiences, and your battle scars to another opportunity. This way of thinking allows you to treat your job choices the same way an investor uses stock options—to gain access to high-return opportunities while minimizing the risk of loss.

The value of a stock option is a product of several variables:

- *Time*. An option's value increases with the time available to exercise the option.

- *Volatility*. How much does the price of the underlying security fluctuate? Because the owner of an option has a right but not an obligation to exercise, option values increase with volatility.

- *Price differential*. How much above or below the current price is the exercise price? The more the option is "in the money" (the exercise price is less than the current price of the underlying security), the greater the value of the option.

In the context of your labor allocation decisions, the time variable refers to the duration of your professional career. The volatility variable refers to the likely ups and downs of the labor markets and the industry in which you work, and the price differential variable refers to the difference between your total compensation at a given time (including all forms of compensation such as salary, bonus, equity incentive, and professional development opportunities) and the market compensation for your skills and responsibilities. Thinking about your job decisions in this framework can lead you to unconventional conclusions. For example, you might conclude that the market rate for your skills is $50,000, but be willing to take a job that pays $40,000 because the "option value" or upside of taking this job—equity ownership, new skills, or access to a rapidly growing industry—compensates you for doing so. This upside need not be only financial: Even if the lower-paying company doesn't turn out to be the next Google, it might represent the best opportunity to develop new marketable skills and build your brand.

■ Key Conclusions

In addition to evaluating the current pros and cons of a job opportunity such as cash compensation and benefits, you should assess how it will positively or negatively affect the value of your personal brand—your perceived qualifications for larger opportunities elsewhere.

Your brand is generally maximized by developing broadly applicable expertise in business functions such as finance, marketing, or general management that can be applied across multiple industries and locations.

A more volatile labor market, combined with the increasing likelihood of a long career, makes the portability of these skills increasingly valuable.

CHAPTER 4

Think Like an Investor When Making Career Decisions

M any of the principles investors use to evaluate the attractiveness of a stock can be applied to an employment decision. When considering a job, think of yourself as an investor. But instead of buying a stock or bond with cash, you are contributing labor in exchange for compensation in the form of salary, experience, and possibly commission, bonus, and stock ownership. You could choose to spend your labor asset among numerous companies that might bid for your labor, so just like an investor, your task is one of identifying relative value. You must prioritize opportunities that provide the best mix of cash compensation, ownership, professional development, and options for different employment in the future.

As I approach my 20-year reunion at Harvard Business School, the implications of thinking like an investor can be seen in the professional choices of my classmates. In this chapter, I offer more than 10 investor criteria, but they can be summarized in the following broad categories: selecting a profession that offers a combination of risks and rewards that accords with your life and family circumstances; identifying markets and businesses that are likely to grow; identifying employers with attractive business models; and identifying opportunities that enhance the personal brand that will broaden your eventual opportunities. A comparison of several classmates' choices highlights the impact these criteria can have on the trajectory of a career.

Before attending Harvard, I had been in the Army, and by the time I graduated from business school, I was married with one child and a lot of debt. So my tolerance for more risk was relatively low, and I had a strong interest in finance. This led me to investment banking in New York, which offered both a relatively low risk of layoffs and high cash compensation for junior professionals. Investment banking is a medium-growth field but possesses a solid business model with consistent profitability and cash flow. It also provided valuable branding or personal franchise skills in finance and investing, as well as access to a vast professional network in Manhattan.

My classmate Susan was single with minimal debt and a strong business pedigree. She had been a McKinsey consultant before going to business school. Given her experiences and risk profile, she opted for a job at an Internet company in San Francisco that ultimately led to a leadership position at Google. While Susan's choice of a relatively untried new company represented some startup risk and lower initial cash compensation, she joined a rapidly growing business with an exceptional business model and access to an unmatched network near Silicon Valley.

John returned to a large retail company where he had worked before going to business school. This choice represented very low risk. Cash compensation was high, and he had worked there before. Growth in the market was relatively low, but the business model was sound and the job offered access to a good but not great business network in New Jersey with access to New York.

Jason was a talented engineer and enjoyed solving real-world problems. He joined a company that made construction equipment. Because of the company's long history of success and good cash pay, this was a low-risk move. But it came with a relatively slow growing, cyclical market, a mediocre business model, and a location in the Midwest that was less than ideal for professional networking.

As we close in on 20 years, all four of us have been successful. But in general, those who embraced more risk, identified businesses with good growth prospects and sound business models, and exploited robust professional networks have accumulated greater wealth. The key differentiator in the accumulation of wealth was not intellect, work ethic, or talent—it was career selection and how the four of us chose to employ our labor assets.

◼ Evaluating the Opportunities

The following paragraphs explain investor principles applicable to making career decisions. While all these principles should be considered, I have attempted to list them in order of importance.

Establish the risk-return profile. When evaluating an opportunity, the first important factor is determining the likely risks and rewards and the key assumptions implicit in that risk-return profile. Just as an investor can make asset-allocation choices among bonds and stocks, job seekers can choose to allocate their labor to opportunities that offer very different patterns of risk and reward. Understanding those patterns is critical for several reasons. First, as we will see later in Section III, the risk-return profile of your job choice has implications for how you manage your financial matters. Furthermore, a clear understanding of that profile allows you to establish criteria up front for an eventual decision to move on to another job. For example, like someone who purchases a bond and begins to perceive high levels of risk in the issuer's business, if you chose a job for its stability and come to see that the company's underperformance is imperiling that stability, you should reconsider your decision. Just as a professional investor develops an investment thesis for a stock (a rationale for why the stock is desirable), you must develop one for your labor choice and force yourself to reexamine the decision and the thesis when circumstances change.

Evaluate the long-term growth potential. For a long-term investor, growth is the largest driver of future value. For an employee, this is even more important. The employee's time horizon—perhaps a 50-year career—is significantly longer than most financial investors', so an employee has more opportunity to benefit from the compounding effects of growth over an extended period. In addition to better pay, growth environments usually provide more noncash compensation—professional opportunity, including more chances for advancement and less likelihood of layoffs. This can transform employees' wealth creation over time. Assume that two friends started with their employers at the same time, each stayed 30 years, each was granted 10,000 stock options at a $10 share price, and each company's stock was valued at 20 times annual earnings. The only difference between the two friends is that the first worked for an emerging technology company that was able to increase earnings at a 10 percent compound annual growth rate over the 30 years while the second worked for a mature company whose earnings grew only 3 percent per year over the same period. Even if the price-to-earnings ratios stay at 20 times earnings over the 30 years, the value of the first employee's options is $1,640,000—12 times the friend's $140,000.

Because long-term growth is difficult to forecast, investors (and employees) should value growth that results from multiple factors more highly than growth from one factor. For example, many technology companies grow rapidly because the market for their products and services soars. But even more attractive, generally, are companies that demonstrate the ability to effectively manage growth not just because their markets expand, but also through multiple channels such as market-share gains, geographic expansion, outsourcing, new product introduction, or successful acquisitions. They are more likely to achieve their long-term objectives even if one source of growth doesn't materialize.

Check the company's capital efficiency. Investors look at numerous measures such as return on equity (ROE), return on assets (ROA), return on invested capital (ROIC) or return on tangible invested capital (ROTIC).* While these measures produce different ratios, they are all attempting to measure how much cash a company produces in relation to how much capital is employed in the business. Of these metrics, I prefer return on tangible invested capital (ROTIC) because it gives the purest picture of a company's cash flows from operations relative to the invested capital required to run the business. While there is no hard and fast rule for investors, good businesses usually generate returns on tangible invested capital above 20 percent, which is comfortably in excess of the cost that lenders and equity investors will likely demand for accepting the risk of investing. This number is important to investors and employees alike because it is a good indicator of how successful a company has been in developing barriers to competition to protect its profits as well as how much investment will be required to expand the business. Businesses with high ROTIC generally require little incremental investment to grow. Apart from ROTIC, the business must be evaluated for both the stability of cash flows and the risk that assets will be lost. If the risks are low, investors are willing to accept a lower ROTIC.

This metric is relevant to employees for several reasons. First, it indicates the value added by the company's services or products. High return on capital suggests a high degree of differentiation from competitors' offerings and high barriers to entry for new rivals. Low returns imply low differentiation. Businesses with high returns on capital are generally, but not always, "asset light," meaning they derive their competitive edge from their people, brand, or intellectual property.

---

* ROTIC equals earnings before interest, taxes, and amortization divided by tangible assets minus cash and current operating liabilities. Tangible assets exclude nonphysical assets such as patents, trademarks, copyrights, goodwill, and brand recognition. Operating liabilities include accounts payable, accrued expenses, and income tax payable.

Second, because their people are a source of differentiation, high-return businesses are more likely to pay key employees well to preserve their competitive advantage. Consider asset-light businesses such as real estate brokerage, investment brokerage, or management consulting in which a company's performance is almost solely dependent upon its people. All these professions compensate their high performers very well. In contrast, a capital-intensive steel mill, utility, or manufacturing company will likely see its main competitive advantage in its investments in assets, processes, and equipment, rather than in people. In such a business, you are likely to find senior leaders who are well compensated for managing this large pool of assets, but the broad employee base probably provides services that are commoditized and therefore not highly paid. When a business experiences challenges—and they all do eventually—I would prefer to work for one that must prioritize investments in its people rather than assets. Finally, high-return businesses are generally less likely to suffer financial distress because they more consistently generate cash flow after servicing all obligations and require less new investment to sustain performance over time.

Look for a robust business model. Investors seek business models that are forgiving when unexpected events occur. So should employees. Invariably, a dynamic marketplace will present surprises, and some businesses are inherently more flexible in reacting. Some points to check:

- *Predictability of revenue.* Long-term market growth rates are the hardest variable for investors to forecast. As a result, investors often prefer businesses that display characteristics that make future revenue more predictable. These include businesses that have recurring revenue (Fidelity mutual funds), businesses that have a significant aftermarket or post-sale component (Caterpillar), businesses widely diversified among customers and geography (FedEx), and businesses that can sustain sales in good and bad economies (Walmart and Coca-Cola, as opposed to purveyors of luxuries like Neiman Marcus).

- *Fixed versus variable costs.* Businesses with a high proportion of variable costs are more able to mitigate booms and busts in revenue. Advisory businesses such as accounting, consulting, and legal firms are great examples of businesses with significant variable costs. Employee and discretionary costs, including travel, subcontractors, and business development, often represent more than 80 percent of their total costs and can be rapidly and dramatically reduced to meet changing demand. You rarely hear of financial distress related to these types of businesses because they can generally prevent losses through rightsizing. Euphemisms aside, these companies often achieve the desired cost reductions by laying off employees. While this may be a good decision for the business, it is less pleasant for the employees. If you're a better than average employee, however, your interests are well aligned with the long-term interests of the company and rightsizing will be less likely to target you.

At the other end of the spectrum, a prominent example of a business with extremely high fixed costs is the airline industry. As demand drops, airlines are hard-put to take out capacity. It's difficult and expensive to eliminate routes and flight schedules; employees are unionized, limiting the ability to reduce the size of the workforce; and the main assets (airplanes) have already been purchased or leased. Revenues drop in hard times as both ticket prices and travel decrease, while expenses remain relatively constant. Given these business model attributes, it's no coincidence that the airline industry has experienced frequent bankruptcies and poor professional opportunities for employees.

■ *Safety of the business assets.* Assets of a business that are short-term in nature, can quickly be converted to cash, possess little risk of *impairment* (financiers' polite term for the loss of much or all of the investment), or are readily salable are generally safer than assets that are long-term, illiquid, or vulnerable to impairment. Staying with our previous business comparison, the primary asset of an advisory firm is accounts receivable (bills to customers), which are by definition readily turned into cash, usually with 30- to 45-day payment terms. The balance sheet produces cash as the business shrinks. By contrast, airplanes, the primary assets of an airline, become difficult to sell when the industry contracts. As the business shrinks, the balance sheet produces little cash to offset losses from operations.

■ *A local service delivery model and minimal risk of technology disruption.* For a potential investor or employee with a long-term perspective, it's important to evaluate how global trade and technology will affect the business. Over decades, it is certain that low-cost regions like China, India, and Mexico will continue to gain share in industries that are relatively labor intensive or where the labor content adds relatively little value, like manufacturing common consumer goods and textiles. Furthermore, continued technology innovation will decrease the "friction" of distance and international trade, making it easier for low-cost countries to compete with our high-cost labor. Therefore, from an employee perspective, I favor businesses that have a local service delivery model, in which the actual service or product must be provided locally, or have characteristics that require significant real-time interaction or collaboration with customers and partners. These industries and job functions are less likely to be harmed by these trends. Examples of professional choices possessing these characteristics include health care, defense, maintenance services, and education.

Favor a conservative capital structure. For an investor, leverage—debt—can be an attractive way to enhance return across a portfolio in which diversification among many companies mitigates risk. Financial leverage in a specific business can also be attractive for investors and senior managers. Because a significant component of their total compensation is related to stock-price appreciation, they stand to be compensated for the incremental risk created by borrowing. However, a highly leveraged balance sheet generally presents an unappealing risk-reward profile for the mass of employees, who receive most of their compensation through wages rather than equity. In essence, the employees are assuming incremental risk that results from leverage without the potential benefits of leveraged equity returns.

Keep stock option terms in perspective. I have had friends tell me they made a career decision about joining a company in part on the basis of the stock price—"My options are at a great strike price." This was probably a misguided decision. For an investor, security price or valuation is one of the most important measures of a desirable investment. In a career decision, however, it is one of the least important factors. An active investor's primary objective is to identify mispricings in the market, exploit the opportunity by investing at a low price, and sell when market participants drive up the stock to a price that accurately reflects the opportunity. Skilled investors evaluate these issues and more to judge whether the stock is correctly priced in relation to its opportunities and risks. But because an employee's time horizon is long and there are more transaction costs associated with switching jobs than selling a stock, valuation, or buy-in point, becomes less relevant. The longer the time horizon, the less important initial valuation becomes.

A memorable example of this is Google. When Google went public, it was still an unproven firm with an unproven business model but with huge potential. In spite of minimal historical performance, the company was valued above $10 billion at the IPO. An investor who possessed equal risk of gain and loss could reasonably conclude that this was not an attractive opportunity, and many did. However, for an employee, the analysis is different. Google offered some exceptional fundamentals, had lots of cash to ensure it would have the opportunity to execute its business plan for at least several years, and offered significant upside to a potential employee through stock options, which carry no risk of loss, and through increased professional opportunity and responsibility in an exploding market. Google, of course, turned out to be a great investment decision for both employee and investor—in 2015, Google was worth nearly $400 billion. But the differing financial and professional risk profiles were real: The investor faced high risk and high return in a volatile situation, while the employee had high return opportunity—lots of room for gains—and minimal financial risk.

Table 4.1 shows how time can trump changes in price-to-earnings ratios (P/Es). Equity investments with high growth and high valuations can produce volatile outcomes for investors who have a relatively short investment horizon (most active managers hold a security for less than 12 months). But over a longer horizon, like that of an employee, initial valuation becomes less relevant and long-term growth becomes the dominant factor driving value, even if the company's P/E declines. This example shows how an investor might lose 50 percent of his money if the P/E contracted from 40 to 15 over the course of a single year, but an employee with a 10-year time horizon could more than double his money in spite of the P/E contraction so long as the business continues to grow.

I caution readers not to draw the wrong conclusion from the Google example. Pursuing a job at Google before its IPO was attractive in spite of significant uncertainty about its stock price because stock-price volatility was the only major risk and there were significant other benefits such as the opportunity to get great experience in a well-funded venture while establishing a powerful personal brand through affiliation with Google and its lucrative, growing markets. This is very different from many startups backed

TABLE 4.1	Time Trumps P/Es		
Holding Period (Years)	Purchase P/E	Compound Earnings Growth	Multiple of Initial Investment If P/E Contracts to 15
1	40	20%	0.5
5	40	20%	0.9
10	40	20%	2.3
25	40	20%	35.8

by venture capitalists in the dot-com era that offered significant operational risk—risk of proving the business model, risk of securing funding—in addition to stock-price volatility.

Employ the concept of portfolio diversification in your labor decisions. Because you can't predict the impact of Murphy's Law (if something can go wrong, it will), a cardinal rule for investors is diversification. This principle has implications for your labor allocation decisions. Don't underestimate the impact of career choices on your family's capacity for later job mobility. Specifically consider the following factors:

- *Breadth of skills.* Broader is better when it comes to job responsibility and the skills you have and will gain. While it may be rewarding and often comfortable to be the expert in a specific area, it can also be limiting: You have implicitly tied your future to the demand for your expertise.

- *Size of industry.* Bigger is better. Since you will likely change jobs more than several times over the course of a career, having a bigger arena to play in allows for more flexibility and mobility.

- *Geography of opportunity.* Bigger is better. Choosing to work in a large metropolitan area allows you to minimize the switching cost of a job change in the future because you are more likely to find an attractive opportunity that does not require moving. Willie Sutton was famously quoted as explaining he robbed banks because that's where the money is. This same principle applies to acquiring wealth the good old-fashioned legal way: If you want to acquire significant wealth, put yourself in an environment that provides significant interaction with those who *have* significant wealth. This is most easily accomplished by living in select pockets of concentrated wealth— the metro areas of New York, Los Angeles, Chicago, Boston, San Francisco, and Washington, D.C.—or through academic affiliation with schools that graduate the highest-income earners such as those in the Ivy League. This strategy is just common sense and acknowledges that success is rarely accomplished alone, so by putting yourself in an environment among aggressive and smart high earners, you are much more likely to ride the wave of collective prosperity. Some advisers caution that the costs of urban living or elite schooling equalize this equation, but I would argue that they are evaluating the payback over an inappropriately short time. The cost of living in these metro areas is daunting to a young professional, but over the course of your half-century career, it can be a relatively small investment compared to the incremental opportunity.

- *Family labor diversification decisions.* While certainly not the primary criterion when a couple makes professional choices, the risks associated with family members working in the same business, or even the same industry, should at least be explicitly acknowledged. The income stream of a couple possessing different jobs in totally different industries is likely to be less volatile than the income stream of a couple both working for the same company or in the same industry. Imagine the unfortunate couples who both worked at Arthur Andersen, Enron, Chrysler, or Lehman Brothers over the past two decades to understand the possible negative implications associated with concentrated labor choices. (If you are in this situation, however, these risks can be mitigated through contingency management and management of the family's capital structure and balance sheet, which is covered in Section IV.)

    Similarly, a couple with one partner in a relatively stable career offering good job security and retirement security, but probably not much chance for big jumps in compensation, is well positioned for the other partner to pursue higher-risk, higher-reward opportunities. In an ideal scenario, one partner's career provides stability and dependable cash flow to cover living expenses while the other's career offers more risk but also a good chance of significant wealth creation. This is sometimes referred to as the spouse bond/equity labor allocation strategy.

Consider your brand in your career decisions. An important part of labor allocation decisions is the impact a decision will have on your personal franchise or brand. Early in a career, acquiring skills and developing your personal brand are critical. Just as a degree from a top institution demonstrates high academic achievement, professional success at a large, well-regarded organization such as General Electric, Goldman Sachs, or Apple goes a long way toward validating a young professional's capabilities. Assuming you have experienced success in your early career, the older you get, the less you need this third-party validation. More personal history should produce a unique personal franchise.

■ Key Conclusions

Most of us incorrectly attribute professional success and wealth creation to hard work and talent. Clearly, success requires these attributes, but wealth creation also requires a work environment conducive to achieving success and wealth. The great business leaders of our time—Bill Gates, Warren Buffett, Larry Ellison—were talented, but they also picked fertile environments to apply their talents. Applying investor principles to your professional decisions can help you identify fertile environments.

The best-informed professional decisions must be evaluated not in isolation, but with consideration of your whole family's professional choices, risk tolerance, and liquidity. Your financial goal is to maximize family wealth, not just individual wealth.

THINK LIKE AN INVESTOR WHEN MAKING CAREER DECISIONS

CHAPTER 5

Don't Overlook Retirement Benefits Just Because They're Not Imminent

No recruiter wants to hear that a job candidate is overly concerned with retirement benefits, yet these benefits should be one of numerous criteria that are part of your framework for making professional decisions. The main distinction to understand is the difference between defined-contribution and defined-benefit pension plans.

As we saw in Chapter 1, defined-benefit plans are rapidly disappearing in the private sector but are still common in government jobs. Even there, though, financially pressed employers are moving away from defined-benefit plans, and employees can be badly hurt by wrong decisions made during plan conversions.

A defined-contribution plan—401(k), 403(b), or similar programs—is generally funded with pre-tax dollars from the employee and in many cases the company. These plans have some attractive features. All contributions made by the employees are their property regardless of future employment. Once the company's vesting requirements* are satisfied, the funds contributed by the company also become the property of the employee. The employee has significant flexibility and control over the investment options and the resulting financial performance. The investments grow and compound on a pre-tax basis, accelerating the wealth creation opportunity. And the value of these assets is perfectly visible at all times, which allows employees to periodically rearrange the investments for adequate financial security upon retirement. For example, employees can change their annual contributions, adjust planned retirement dates, or change investment strategy based on new information over time. The primary drawback of this plan is simple: Employees assume the risk that the investments they choose will do poorly, putting them in danger of outliving their assets.

By contrast, in a traditional defined-benefit pension plan, the employer promises a specific level of benefits and assumes responsibility for funding this liability regardless of how the investments perform and how long the employee lives. However, five characteristics of a defined-benefit program can significantly decrease the expected value to the employee.

1. *A risk of not qualifying.* In today's job markets characterized by free agency and labor mobility, the lack of portability decreases the expected value. An employee may well leave, voluntarily or involuntarily, before qualifying for any retirement benefits. Vesting rules for retirement benefits are governed by each company's plan documents, but plans can require up to five years to qualify for any benefits and up to seven years to earn 100 percent of the promised benefit. (While employer contributions in a defined-contribution plan are also subject to vesting rules, the employee contributions belong to the employee immediately.)

2. *Varying schedules of accumulation of benefits.* Even if the anticipated benefits from a defined-contribution and defined-benefit plan are roughly the same, the rates at which employees accumulate benefits differ dramatically. Most defined-benefit plans' payouts are based on a formula biased toward final average pay—the pension benefit grows substantially faster in the later years of a career than in the early years, in what is known as a J-shaped accrual pattern. The result is that employees who quit or are fired essentially subsidize

---

*The time before the employee has nonforfeitable rights to the company's contributions, which ranges from immediately to five years' employment.

those who stay. This is a retention tool for the company but a deterrent for an employee who wishes to maximize career mobility. By contrast, a defined-contribution plan grows in a more linear fashion, and you take your share with you whenever you leave.

3. *A risk that the rules will change over time.* A company can't reduce the part of a pension that has already been earned, but it may at any time change the rate at which the benefit is earned in the future. The company can change the rules halfway through your career. With pension benefits disproportionately earned toward the end of a career, the cost of switching jobs or plans at that point is likely to be high.

4. *A risk that the plan will fail.* You must also weigh the likelihood that your company's plan will be able to satisfy its obligations. Numerous pension plans have failed despite federal regulations requiring companies to contribute enough to ensure financial viability. When the obligations of a plan exceed the capacity to pay, the plan will likely be taken over by the federal Pension Benefit Guaranty Corporation (PBGC). However, the payment from the PBGC is limited to $59,300 per year for a worker who retires at 65 and is usually substantially less. Worse, the PBGC itself is arguably not financially sound. It consistently runs a multibillion-dollar deficit. While pension plan failures are still relatively rare, the negative consequences are so large that they deserve consideration.

5. *Inability to direct unused benefits for the benefit of your legacy.* As we discussed in Chapter 1, a lesser but still important objective of your financial planning activities is to manage your assets for the benefit of your family or causes of your choosing when you die. While a defined-benefit program guarantees that you, and possibly your spouse, can't outlive your benefit, it generally has zero value upon death and is therefore of less benefit to your estate.

■ Obstacles to Planning

Defined-benefit plans create two significant financial planning challenges. The first is the inability to effectively value the expected benefit. The proceeds of a defined-benefit plan are a product of many variables: the stated pension benefit; the likelihood that the employee will vest or make it to full retirement; the likelihood that the company will change the benefit levels during the course of a career; the likelihood that the plan and the company will be financially able to satisfy the obligations to retirees decades in the future; and the distant-future payout policy of the PBGC if the plan and company fail to meet their obligations.

The other major challenge is that once you have spent significant years earning credits in a defined-benefit plan, it becomes difficult and expensive to change employers. Consider someone who has worked for a company for 25 years and can retire with full benefits in another 10 years, but over those past 25 years both the company and its pension plan have become financially shaky. That employee is on the wrong end of the J-curve. Staying the last 10 years is compelling because leaving is punitive, so probably the best alternative is to stay put and hope for the best. In recent history, hope has often proved to be a bad strategy. With a defined-*contribution* plan, however, employees can vote with their feet, taking their retirement assets with them to seek greener pastures.

Fundamentally, the choice between the two retirement approaches comes down to how much you value control and what risks you are comfortable assuming. I am more comfortable with the risks associated with the defined-contribution option because it gives the employees the flexibility to maximize their labor assets by pursuing the best opportunities throughout a career. This choice also makes the value of retirement assets more transparent at every stage of a career, allowing employees to adjust planned savings, retirement age, and spending patterns as needed. Finally, while many employees highly value the certainty of a defined monthly pension promised by defined-benefit plans, an investment portfolio can be constructed to provide similar monthly income with less risk. We explore this topic more thoroughly in Section III.

▪ Key Conclusions

Consideration of retirement benefits, however distant, has a place in career decisions.

Each type of pension plan has its own risks—in a defined-contribution plan, these include the risks of poor investment choices and outliving your income; in a defined-benefit plan, the risks of unexpected changes in benefit terms, possible inability of the plan or company to pay the promised pension, and constraints on your job mobility.

For those prepared to accept the risks, defined-contribution plans offer valuable flexibility in personal financial planning, career opportunities, investments, and visibility of personal assets.

CHAPTER 6

Complement Your Career Decisions with Insurance

My father has been one of my primary teachers regarding financial decisions, and on most financial topics we agree. However, on purchasing insurance we could not be more different. Dad seems to want to insure *everything* while I want to insure as little as possible. In my view, Dad overinsures his risks by buying life insurance on every member of the family, buying long-term health-care insurance for himself and Mom, and having very comprehensive liability and auto insurance policies. I believe these choices are driven by a fundamental difference in approach. Dad is trying to buy peace of mind so that when something bad happens, he knows there will be no negative (and sometimes even positive) financial implications. I, on the other hand, view insurance as a necessary evil. To me, insurance is a loser's game with the expected payout always less than the expected future value of the premiums paid had I invested the money until needed to fund the insurable event. So I attempt to self-insure as much as possible and buy insurance only to protect against catastrophic events that could impoverish the family. My approach might result in some unexpected costs, but I also expect it to result in a higher return on my investment.

Whatever your personal bias, in addition to making investments to maximize the value of your labor, you must make investments to protect your labor assets—your ability to work. These investments are primarily in the form of insurance. If we refer back to our initial discussion of Family Inc. Net Worth in Chapter 1, the young man has approximately $2 million in expected after-tax labor assets at age 25. At this point in his career, he probably needs the most insurance to ensure that if some unlikely disaster—a serious illness, a major accident—dramatically reduces his labor assets, he receives enough incremental financial assets (money) to make up for the lost potential income from his labor. While there are numerous types of insurance, three are relevant in protecting Family Inc. Each is designed to eliminate the going-out-of-business scenario that could bankrupt you and your family.

Long-term disability insurance. This product is designed to replace a significant portion of your salary should illness or injury make you unable to perform your job. You need this type of insurance until permanently stopping work doesn't impose financial hardship on you or your family. This is the most important insurance need because when an event seriously impairs your ability to work, you not only lose labor potential but you still require significant consumption—you become a financial liability to your family. Financially, this is worse than dying!

So disability coverage is the one form of insurance no working adult can afford to do without. The risks and consequences you are assuming without disability insurance are clear in a few statistics: 25 percent of today's 20-year-olds will become disabled before they retire, and medical problems contributed to 62 percent of all personal bankruptcies and half of all home foreclosures even before the last economic downturn.

In spite of these dire statistics, most Americans remain uninsured; 69 percent of private sector employees have no long-term disability insurance other than Social Security Disability Insurance. SSDI is inadequate, with over 65 percent of initial claims denied in 2012 and average monthly benefits of $1,130 per month for those unlucky enough to need it but lucky enough to qualify. Private disability insurance represents the best way to protect your family from financial harm when your biggest asset, your labor, is unexpectedly impaired. All adults, no matter what their age or family situation, should carry this type of insurance until they have accumulated enough financial assets to fund their consumption for the rest of their lives through returns on and sales of capital assets.

Key criteria to consider when evaluating long-term disability policies include renewability; how the insurer defines total disability and "residual disability"; built-in exclusions; each insurance company's financial stability; and price. Detailed discussion of these criteria is outside the scope of this book, but my general recommendation is to maximize areas of the policy related to ensuring payment: Once the policy is in place, it should remain in place for as long as you desire; the policy's definition of disability should be broad; benefits should continue for a long period, such as until age 65; and the insurance company should have a top rating from a credit-rating agency such as A.M. Best, Moody's, or Standard & Poor's. If you are price conscious, I recommend compromising on the total coverage amount as well as accepting a longer elimination period—how long you'd have to wait before payments begin. These compromises are consistent with the goal of preventing family bankruptcy.

Long-term disability policies are occasionally provided as an employee benefit. Regardless of who buys the insurance, if the premiums are paid with after-tax dollars, then the benefits are tax free.

Life insurance. Life insurance, also a critical component of your financial plan, provides income replacement for your family should you die unexpectedly. While both term life and whole life insurance programs have their merits (whole life possesses an investment component), separating the insurance program from the investment program with term life results in lower costs and more flexibility, and is generally the superior option.* The following are relevant considerations when constructing your life insurance program.

- If the goal is income replacement for your family, then life insurance is generally not required by young adults or couples. While the death of a spouse or partner can be tragic, it does not necessarily create financial hardship unless the couple has incurred significant liabilities where income replacement would be required to satisfy these ongoing obligations. The most common events that should trigger young adults to evaluate the need for insurance are purchasing a home with a mortgage and having children. Until that time, life insurance is generally a poor investment.

- Couples with children often procure insurance products to mitigate losses of income when the primary earner dies or becomes disabled, but many neglect to buy insurance for the primary child caregiver. I encourage couples to insure a way of life in addition to a loss of potential labor income. Having additional financial resources

*Whole life is generally more appropriate for families who are likely to encounter a tax liability upon death because of the size of their estates. In this circumstance, the insurance serves as a guaranteed source of liquidity to pay taxes due on inherited assets that may not be easily turned into cash. This is discussed in greater detail in Chapter 26.

to support raising a family if the main caregiver dies or becomes disabled will be important during such challenging circumstances, no matter how much or little that partner was earning.

- The most cost-effective life insurance program is generally what's known as a ladder structure—a group of term policies with terms that end at different stages throughout your working life and simulate your depleting labor asset over time. Figure 6.1 shows how a ladder of policies might work for our 25-year-old man's $2 million lifetime labor asset (his expected earnings), as charted in Chapter 1, Figure 1.1. At each age, the policies still in force reflect the remaining expected earnings. For example, Figure 6.1 shows that from ages 25 to 30, his death benefit would be approximately $2 million and from ages 30 to 40, the benefit would decrease to $1.5 million, mimicking the value of his remaining labor.

Umbrella Insurance. The third pillar of a sound insurance program is an umbrella policy. This covers the risk of legal actions against you, your family, or your property. While disability and life insurance protect your labor asset and replace lost income, an umbrella policy protects your accumulated financial assets. Therefore, while the other insurance amounts will likely go down over time, this coverage will increase as your assets grow. Given the relatively low price for this type of coverage, I generally recommend a minimum of $1 million in coverage, with increases over time as your Family Inc. Net Worth increases.

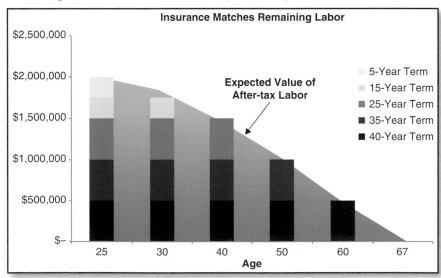

FIGURE 6.1 Term Life Insurance Ladder

■ How Needs Evolve

My own experience and plans may illuminate how these insurance programs and needs change over a lifetime. While everybody's situation is unique, my insurance needs have evolved in a reasonably typical way as my family and financial circumstances have changed.

Early adulthood. In my twenties, I had little money, little debt, and few assets, and my wife and I were both educated and gainfully employed. Thus, I had little need for insurance. While my death would have been tragic for my wife, it would have caused minimal financial hardship. We had only three types of insurance: disability, umbrella liability, and auto. Essentially, the only risks that could bankrupt the family were risks of one of us becoming disabled or being sued, or risks related to damages caused by our driving.

Approaching middle age. By the time I was in my early thirties, our circumstances had changed dramatically. I was earning substantially more money and I was starting to accumulate meaningful wealth, but I had also incurred significant debt through investments in education, a home, and cars. My wife no longer worked, and we had the pleasure and additional financial responsibilities of two children. I now had real needs for insurance—were I to die or lose my ability to work, my family would have faced hardship. During this period of my life, I had a legitimate need for term life insurance as well as disability, umbrella, and auto insurance. Not only did the kinds of insurance increase, the amounts increased dramatically to replicate my earnings and satisfy the family's increased liabilities, spending needs, and assets that would require protection should I be sued.

Empty nesters. My wife and I will soon enter yet another stage in our insurance needs. My income hasn't changed substantially, but over the years I have acquired enough wealth to support us through our lifetimes, assuming reasonable investment returns and spending. At the same time, our obligations are decreasing. Our kids will be young adults and increasingly self-sufficient. Our debts have decreased substantially, and my wife is free to rejoin the workforce. In these new circumstances, our disability and life insurance needs will go down while umbrella, auto, and possibly long-term-care insurance needs will grow with our assets, cars, and increasing ages.

Most couples face these three stages to some degree. For the lucky who acquire significant wealth, there is likely a fourth stage that I term *legacy management*. Insurance can be a valuable tool to manage the estate tax liability when you die. We cover this in greater detail in Chapter 25.

■ Key Conclusions

Every family has labor and financial assets that must be used to fund the obligations it incurs over a lifetime. Insurance is an important tool to protect these assets from catastrophic loss.

Common forms of appropriate insurance include life, disability, umbrella, long-term health care, and auto. In the right circumstances, all are appropriate risk management tools. But they are not designed to be good investments and therefore should be bought sparingly.

Insurance should be purchased in an amount that reflects the potential loss to Family Inc. Its purpose isn't to create a windfall.

MANAGE YOUR ASSETS LIKE A CFO MANAGES A BUSINESS

In Section II, we covered concepts that can be employed to maximize the value of your labor assets. Section III shows how to maximize your family's financial assets while minimizing the likelihood of financial distress.

CHAPTER 7

Your Financial Assets Serve Many Functions in Your Family Business

There is a broad misconception that asset management is the same thing as investing. In fact, these are two distinct activities requiring different skills. I would argue that anyone reading this book has the ability to be a good asset manager, but very few will be good investors.

Asset management encompasses the Family CFO's ability to effectively manage *all* the family's assets to meet the family's needs. It includes responsibilities like ensuring you have saved for a rainy day or an unexpected event, effectively purchasing and financing the goods your family requires, managing your career, and planning for retirement. Investing is a much narrower endeavor: buying assets like stocks and bonds to generate a profit.

My father is a classic case in point—he has been a great family asset manager and a pretty mediocre investor. Dad effectively managed his career, managed the family assets to ensure our needs were met, and effectively planned for retirement. However, when it came to investments, he couldn't avoid the temptations of active management. Dad just loved the process of investing and as a result was a willing buyer for anyone who could pitch the merits of an investment opportunity. Stan, Dad's broker, had lots of "good ideas" complemented by whatever Dad read in *Fortune*, *Forbes*, or the *Wall Street Journal* that week and, of course, whatever Warren Buffett said was a good investment. My father will tell you that in the aggregate, his investments have made money, which is true—most investments do with enough time—but I highly doubt they have performed as well as a simple broad market index over the same period.

Active investing for individuals is analogous to a joke about how good the technology is on new airplanes these days. Instead of two pilots, these new airplanes require one pilot and one dog. The dog's job is to bite the pilot if he tries to touch the controls.

Many of us would be better off if we had a dog around to bite us when we are tempted to actively manage our investments. Good investment performance is more often achieved by what we don't do than what we do.

■ The Elements of Asset Management

Before developing a specific asset management investment program, let's review the key functions that your asset management business serves. The six primary functions of your asset management business are to:

1. *Provide a safety net when your labor business underperforms.* Your asset management business can provide a critical source of funds when your labor business underperforms—when you are paid less than anticipated or lose your job. While the Family Inc. Net Worth chart in Figure 1.1 assumes constant employment at growing real rates of pay—a reasonable assumption over the long term—the unfortunate reality is that a family's income is often more erratic in the short term. In volatile times, your assets serve as a valuable buffer to support required consumption. Your assets will, hopefully, provide this safety net just a few times over a long and prosperous career, but though it may come up rarely, this is the most important role of your asset management business. An adage among bankruptcy lawyers is that companies often go bankrupt not because they are worth less than their liabilities but because they run out of cash. This same principle applies to individuals: Having adequate liquidity through cash reserves, available credit, and liquid investments is the best way to avoid financial distress. If

given enough time, an effective Family CFO can overcome significant setbacks from capital losses or temporary underemployment by working longer than planned, increasing savings, or reducing consumption. But traumatic financial distress—bankruptcy—is hard to surmount.

2. *Provide short-term liquidity to manage Family Inc.* This is essentially a banking function in which your asset management business provides capital or "float" to bridge the timing differences between funds coming in and funds going out. Examples include paying annual school tuition at the beginning of the year, prepaying premiums for insurance, or funding your 401(k) for the year. Over time, investments of this type should be neutral as they essentially serve the same purpose as overdraft protection on a checking account: You'll pay them back.

3. *Acquire business and consumption assets.* Your asset management business is also the funding source, or at least the collateral required for borrowing, for the purchase of all types of significant assets— long-term depreciating assets such as vehicles and computers, and assets that are intended to appreciate rather than depreciate, such as education, stocks, and real estate.

4. *Accumulate wealth.* The fundamental objective of your investment management business is to increase assets through a comprehensive investment program. This activity is similar to managing your own diversified mutual fund with the simple goal of investment appreciation and income from dividends, interest, and other distributions.

5. *Pay for consumption when your labor assets are exhausted.* When you retire, voluntarily or not, the objective of your asset management business changes to both investment for appreciation and liquidation of assets for consumption. This is more similar to an endowment or pension program that must generate adequate cash flow to support financial obligations and desired spending in addition to achieving its investment objectives.

6. *Fund the seed capital for the next generation of family businesses.* Ultimately, for those who accumulate more financial resources than they consume, these resources serve as start-up capital for the next generation of Family Inc. As is discussed in Chapter 23, when

invested wisely, a small amount of seed capital can dramatically change the next generation's Family Inc. Net Worth.

■ Key Conclusions

As Family CFO, your job is *much* broader than making investment decisions, which is the typical role of investment advisers.

The capital in your asset management business has a significant influence on your ability to raise cash at various and sometimes unexpected times and consequently on how you should allocate your assets.

Your priorities should be to arrange your assets to protect against financial distress and provide for required spending, expand and support your labor business, and only then to make investments to support future consumption. This broad mandate is one of several reasons this critical function cannot be fully outsourced.

CHAPTER 8

Diversify Your Family Business with the Right Investments

When I was seven years old, my father bought me AT&T stock for Christmas. Needless to say, this was a letdown, and I made clear in no uncertain terms that stock had been nowhere on my Christmas list. His response? If I didn't like the stock, I was welcome to sell it and buy whatever I wanted with the money.

Fortunately, I didn't get around to selling my Christmas present for several months—and by the time I looked at it, the stock was up 25 percent. The light bulb went off for me that day, and so began my love affair with investing: Making money without working sounded pretty good to me! With my newfound wealth, my father and I went to see his stockbroker to get a tip for my next investment, funded from my paper route money.

Almost swallowed by the big leather chair in his office, I sat across from my dad's adviser, Stan, as he explained as best he could in seven-year-old terms the concepts of risk, diversification, and the benefits of a portfolio of investments. Given my new knowledge and based on Stan's advice, I promptly bought a certificate of deposit that guaranteed a 7 percent return for the next five years. How could I go wrong? I was guaranteed to make money. And I was reassured when my father commended my choice, saying that he, too, had a fixed-interest portfolio recommended by Stan.

It would take me years, lots of schooling, and lots of lost opportunity to realize that Stan's advice to both me and my dad was flawed because it didn't account for the big picture. Stan helped us create a portfolio that minimized big swings in value on an annual basis, but he didn't help either of us maximize the value of our investments over the very long term (greater than 10 years) when we will need this money during retirement. Neither my father nor I has ever sold our AT&T stock, and given this long time horizon, we would have both been far better off to have bought more stocks instead of CDs and bonds.

Over time, being in the right classes of investments for your situation and needs usually affects results more than picking the right individual securities. Skillful asset allocation—distributing investable funds among the various *types* of investments—is probably the surest route to achieving attractive returns on family investments without undue risk. The challenge, of course, is how to get the choices right.

Investment professionals and academics have assembled a mountain of research and conventional advice on asset allocation that the Family CFO should be aware of. Aware, but skeptical. Understanding investments in the overall context of Family Inc., the CFO will want to modify, or ignore, a lot of the conventional rules of thumb. That's because most conventional approaches look only at financial assets and ignore the value tied up in your house and in your future payments from work and Social Security. You have to factor in these assets to get an accurate picture of the whole pie before you can intelligently carve up the pie into slices of stocks, bonds, and other assets.

■ Strategic Asset Allocation: How to Arrange the Big Picture

What's optimal for particular investors depends on four things: (1) what they can reasonably expect to earn from their investments (their "targeted return"); (2) their present and predicted earnings; (3) their present and predictable future financial obligations; and (4) their time horizon, or duration (when, if ever, will I need to sell these assets?). All these are important considerations, but your time horizon is by far the most influential in determining how best to allocate your investments.

In addition to achieving desired returns, sound investment strategies attempt to minimize leaps and dives in the value of the portfolio. The financial term for these gyrations is *volatility*. It's the primary measure of risk, and it can be reduced through diversification—by investing in asset classes, industries, and geographical areas that tend not to rise and fall at the same time; in financial lingo, they demonstrate low correlation.

Asset classes are groupings of investments that are correlated, meaning that they generally behave similarly over time in measures of three kinds of risk: (1) volatility (how much the value will fluctuate), (2) illiquidity (how easy or hard it might be to sell them when you need the cash), and (3) impairment (loss of capital). The more risk investors assume, the higher the required return.

Cash and near-cash (an asset class including pocket cash, checking and money-market accounts, CDs, and Treasury bills) are unlikely to gyrate or become worthless or hard to sell, but they're equally unlikely to provide big gains. Bonds are somewhat riskier and somewhat likelier to appreciate. At the other extreme, hedge funds, private equity, and other investments requiring very large commitments of capital can return the most when things go right, but are also at the extremes of all three risks. A bit less profitable over time, but considerably less risky, are equities (stocks, stock mutual funds, and exchange-traded funds).

If you embrace risk to achieve higher returns, you may have a bumpy ride. However, with appropriate diversification *and* the ability to manage some illiquidity and volatility along the way, investors are generally well-compensated for the risks. Warren Buffett has put it this way: "Charlie [Munger, his longtime partner] and I would much rather earn a lumpy 15 percent over time than a smooth 12 percent."

Theories of asset allocation are based on two key real world observations:

1. It's hard to predict which asset classes will perform best in a given period.

2. Because asset classes historically have often not behaved alike, diversification can result in less volatility or risk without compromising returns.

For example, based on history, a 10 percent decrease in the U.S. stock markets is likely to be accompanied by smaller drops in many other types of assets: a 9.5 percent decrease in global stocks, a 7.4 percent decrease in hedge funds, a 5.5 percent decrease in emerging-markets bonds, a 2.8 percent decrease in U.S. investment-grade bonds, and only a 1.9 percent decrease in foreign currencies. All of these asset classes are positively correlated (they tend to move in the same direction), but since they don't all move with the same magnitude, they can dampen the portfolio's volatility.

These historical correlations change over time. In general, globalization among the world's economies has produced increased correlations among global stocks, reducing the benefits of diversification. And because of measurement errors, the gains and losses of certain asset classes—private equity, real estate, and so-called absolute return strategies (hedge funds and merger arbitrage funds)—are probably more correlated than they look. Regardless, strategies that pursue uncorrelated asset classes offer a valuable opportunity to reduce volatility without reducing expected return. That's always good.

The stock market in any country will show relatively big annual price swings. But this volatility decreases dramatically as stocks from additional countries are added to an investment portfolio. A statistical analysis covering the entire twentieth century found, for example, that including stocks from 16 countries instead of just one reduced volatility by more than 40 percent in a sample portfolio. That study included only equities of developed international markets. The benefits of diversification would have been even greater with the addition of less correlated asset classes, including emerging-market stocks.

Based on these observations, asset-allocation models recommend broad exposure to numerous markets and asset classes, providing diversification and mitigating the portfolio's volatility while producing the most lucrative risk-adjusted returns—the money that will support your retirement, your gifts, and your dreams for your family.

■ The Conventional Asset-Allocation Models

Because each investor's time horizon and risk appetite are unique, there is no right asset allocation for everybody. However, the following outline is representative of the consensus among most financial advisers for a 40-year-old with a normal tolerance for risk.

- 60 percent equities, consisting of:
    - 35 percent U.S. equities
    - 20 percent international developed-country equities
    - 5 percent emerging-market equities

- 35 percent bonds

- 5 percent cash and near-cash equivalents

Investors seeking real estate exposure commonly dilute their equity exposure by up to 10 percentage points to make room for that asset class, often in the form of real estate investment trusts (REITs), and investors seeking commodity exposure often dilute their fixed income exposure by up to 5 points. Beyond this, institutional investors and high-net-worth individuals often reserve up to 15 percent of their allocations to include alternative assets such as private equity and absolute return or hedge strategies. Practically speaking, gaining access to the latter markets is difficult for individuals with less than $5 million in investable assets, so these strategies are usually excluded from mainstream financial models.

Furthermore, advisers generally recommend an increasing bias toward liquid and fixed income assets as individuals age. A common rule of thumb is that fixed income should represent roughly your current age as a percentage of your portfolio (that is, fixed income would represent 40 percent of your portfolio when you are 40 and 60 percent of your portfolio when you are 60).

■ Weaknesses of the Conventional Models

I strongly advocate employing an asset-allocation model when constructing an investment portfolio, but I believe it should be done in the context of the Family Inc. Net Worth framework presented in Chapter 1. The conventional asset-allocation model described here has significant shortcomings when viewed in this framework. These shortcomings include:

The conventional allocation model focuses on the smoothing effect cash and fixed income has on portfolio volatility but fails to acknowledge that your asset management business also serves an important liquidity function: supplying cash to finance significant business or personal assets, and cash to support your consumption until you are paid for work that you have already provided or while you wait to liquidate other assets. This part of the portfolio serves as the family overdraft account to manage daily cash needs. Given this primary function, the highly liquid investments required to meet these needs are best quantified in absolute dollar amounts, not percentages of a portfolio. Cash allocation decisions should be based on monthly spending patterns and the likelihood you will need to tap these reserves, not on a percentage target of your financial assets. You don't spend percentages.

The conventional model fails to acknowledge the holistic nature of net worth, as defined by our Family Inc. Net Worth concept, which includes the expected after-tax value of labor as the largest asset for most people. When productively employed, labor assets generally produce after-tax cash flows—paychecks, bonuses, stock option gains—that are similar to a bond or annuity: They provide a small amount of income every year relative to the total value, and income from year to year generally does not change significantly. While this income stream is not contractually guaranteed like a bond, the value of its cumulative cash flows is relatively stable over a lifetime, especially when insurance is employed to mitigate the risk of disability or other labor impairment, as discussed in Chapter 6. Furthermore, your Social Security benefits and wages have effectively zero correlation with other financial assets and so provide further benefits of diversification. The magnitude and diversification benefits of labor and Social Security for Family Inc. dramatically reduce the volatility of the family's asset portfolio, and therefore the need to augment the portfolio with assets offering lower risks and lower expected returns, such as bonds, commodities, real estate, and cash.

This allocation model fails to acknowledge that in addition to labor and investment securities, many families own their primary residence, which generally represents their single largest asset other than labor. When this asset is included in our asset-allocation framework, it becomes clear that incremental investments in real estate (rental properties, vacation properties, or even commercial REITs) are not prudent for many families, given their existing concentration in real estate.

The allocation model fails to acknowledge the debt that exists in most family balance sheets related to real estate, education, and consumption items such as vehicles and credit cards. While I advocate employing debt to enhance equity returns in certain circumstances, it does introduce incremental volatility into the Family Inc. Net Worth and must be considered in the context of the overall composition of Family Inc. Net Worth and the Family Inc. Balance Sheet. Debt from your school loans has the same impact on your Family Inc. Balance Sheet as does borrowing money to buy more stocks. Debt is debt.

The allocation model does not account for assets a family may have at the time of retirement from Social Security or a defined-benefit pension plan, both of which act like bonds.

Most traditional asset-allocation models are inappropriately U.S.-centric in their equity allocations. Many advisers recommend that U.S. equities represent 60 percent or more of total equity holdings. This recommendation is dated and backward looking. Today, U.S. equities represent about half the global market capitalization, and the United States comprises less than 25 percent of the global economy, a percentage that has been consistently decreasing as emerging markets such as China, Brazil, and India grow more quickly. Basing your equity allocations on relative global market capitalization values will ensure that your allocations change with the changing dynamics of these economies.

Asset-allocation models frequently underestimate how long you'll hold the investments before you cash them in, if ever. Most advisers recommend an unnecessarily conservative move toward lower-volatility and lower-return assets such as bonds as you age. Increasing exposure to less volatile securities for investments that will be liquidated in the short term is legitimate, but it should be based on the dollar amounts of both expected spending and the Family Inc. Net Worth. These two factors materially affect the time line over which an investor will be forced to cash in significant portions of the portfolio.

In most traditional asset-allocation models, age is the primary variable that influences risk tolerance   as age increases, risk tolerance decreases. In reality, this is such a small part of the story. To highlight this shortcoming, let's compare my father and me.

Dad is 79 and is a retired educator. He has a defined-benefit pension plan that he paid into for over 50 years, and he funds substantially all his consumption from his pension and Social Security. In addition to these, he has multiple homes and real estate holdings, with minimal debt on these properties. Because Dad was a public servant, he has never accumulated significant liquid wealth beyond his pension and real estate, but he has some investments in stocks, bonds, and mutual funds, totaling less than 20 percent of his Family Inc. Net Worth.

My financial picture looks very different. While I am much younger at 46, I have substantially more financial risk inherent in my life. As a business owner, I don't receive a monthly paycheck. I share profits with my partners at the end of the year. My income is heavily influenced by the performance of our investments—my earnings can fluctuate over 500 percent between a good year and a bad year. A really bad year can result in negative cash flow. I also own two houses, both of which have mortgages, and I have two kids who will be college eligible in the next five years. Traditional asset allocation would suggest that Dad should minimize the risk in his investments and I should embrace it. I would argue exactly the opposite. In spite of Dad's age, he is ideally positioned to embrace equity exposure with all assets other than his pension, Social Security, and real estate. I, on the other hand, already have lots of volatility in my annual earnings and considerable debt, so arguably should be more risk averse.

■ A Wealth Effect

As wealth increases, the traditional asset-allocation model breaks down. Assume, for example, that a 67-year-old woman retires with no debts, $500,000 in cash and short-term securities, $500,000 in bonds, $500,000 in real estate, and $3 million in equities. Her after-tax consumption is approximately $150,000 a year. Conventional wisdom suggests she is significantly overweighted to equities and she should sell approximately 50 percent of her equity holdings. This conclusion is wrong for several reasons. First, assuming consistent consumption patterns, this woman will never deplete her net worth, as her assets are likely to grow faster than her consumption. Second, given her rate of consumption relative to her anticipated asset growth, the expected duration on her investments is actually very long in spite of her age. Therefore, rebalancing toward a traditional "safe" fixed income portfolio robs her of a significant long-term compounding opportunity with equities. And the rebalancing is tax inefficient relative to the status quo—bond interest is taxable, and rebalancing often triggers capital gains. Furthermore, as we will see from our history lesson in Chapter 10, this allocation toward bonds will not reduce the long-term ups and downs of her after-tax purchasing power.

Even in our base Family Inc. Net Worth scenario—which assumes retirement at 67; accumulation of about $570,000 in savings; and exhaustion of all assets by age 90—the time horizon for expected equity sales remains relatively distant. Assuming an annual return of 5.0 percent after inflation, taxes, and fees, the savings would generate $42,000 of cash annually during those 23 years. In this scenario, it would take 10 years before those sales depleted even 30 percent of the portfolio.

Let's return to Dad and me, with our different circumstances, and evaluate the impact of our personal situations on how long we expect to hold our investments. Conventional theory would suggest that Dad, at 79, would have a relatively short duration on his investments. In reality, I suspect he will never sell these investments during his lifetime. Because his consumption is fully funded through his pension, Social Security, and real estate investment income, he has no need to sell his investments to maintain his lifestyle. Even with all the risk in my family situation, I, too, am very unlikely to sell equities anytime in the near future. I maintain one year's worth of cash reserves to cover unanticipated emergencies but try to keep the rest of my assets invested. Over the whole of my professional career, I have never reduced my exposure to the markets in any year. My father and I have certainly sold lots of stocks along the way, but neither of us has ever been a net seller—that is, we sold IBM to buy Apple, not to switch into less risky bonds or consume. For anyone who has the liquidity—the disposable cash—to fund investments for future rather than near-term consumption, the duration is likely to be sufficiently long to justify owning equities.

Figures 8.1 and 8.2 compare the impacts of following or modifying the conventional asset allocation. In our scenario, the family of our 40-year-old man has accumulated approximately $76,000 in assets. Employing the traditional asset-allocation model would result in the recommended asset allocations shown in Figure 8.1.

This myopic view of asset allocation, however, which considers only financial assets, produces less than optimal results. Using the same recommended investments from the traditional allocation model in dollar

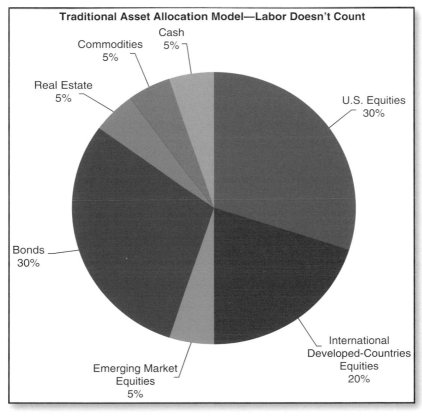

FIGURE 8.1 Asset Allocation for 40-Year-Old

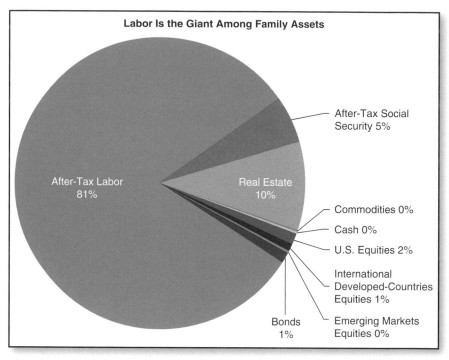

FIGURE 8.2 Family Inc. Net Worth Asset Allocation Model (for 40-year Old)

amounts, but employing the expanded definition of Family Inc. Net Worth, including after-tax labor potential, after-tax Social Security, and a primary residence, we get this very different asset-allocation profile, as shown in Figure 8.2.

Figure 8.2 demonstrates that most family businesses are overallocated toward labor assets—and you can't diversify away from labor assets except by depleting them. We discuss specific actions to address the inadequacies of the traditional asset-allocation model in Chapter 16, but at this point, suffice it to say that the traditional strategic allocation model is badly flawed.

■ Tactical Asset Allocation

In addition to strategic allocation recommendations, investment advisers and institutions frequently suggest an overlay of tactical allocation. If strategic allocations can be thought of as a road map toward reaching long-term financial goals, tactical allocations represent short-term detours, often best avoided. Tactical allocations are generally modest movements around strategic asset-allocation targets—often 5 or 10 percentage points in either direction—based on an assessment of the relative attractiveness of various asset classes. In practice, these are recommendations to modify the percentage targets for an asset class based on a view of the near-term prospects for that asset class, a form of market timing.

While tactical asset allocation is emotionally appealing—wouldn't it have been nice if we could have predicted the Internet bubble of 2000, the credit bubble of 2007, and the commodity bubble of 2008? —the underlying models used to predict asset-class performance, upon which decisions are made, are complex and questionable. They include abstruse econometric models drawing on asset-class yields, macroeconomic signals, fundamental-value signals, and momentum and sentiment signals.

Evidence is scarce that these models are predictive or helpful to the investor, and tactical asset-allocation strategies usually result in incremental expenses and taxes. Finally, the cost of being "not invested" based on tactical asset-allocation recommendations can be high. Equity markets often show material single-day movements, both positive and negative. Research by Vanguard over 15 years demonstrates that the 10 best and worst days represented 30 percent and 33 percent, respectively, of the total return for the period. In other words, two days out of every thousand accounted for approximately 30 percent of the total return—two days you might miss because of a market-timing strategy. The magnitude of these quick movements implies they were likely a product of some exogenous factor—9/11, Lehman Brothers' bankruptcy—and therefore probably unpredictable through macroeconomic signals.

■ Asset Classes with Unique Characteristics

Before we move on from asset-allocation and correlation concepts, it's worth discussing in a little more detail two asset classes that, unlike equities and bonds, may *not* be appropriate in a Family CFO's portfolio.

Commodities. Many traditional asset-allocation models include commodities as a component of the portfolio. Commodities such as precious metals, oil, gas, and crops, are considered attractive investments because they demonstrate little correlation with stocks and bonds, and they perform well in inflationary environments. However, for the Family Inc. portfolio, I do not recommend the inclusion of commodities for two reasons:

(1) commodities by definition appreciate only on a change of intrinsic value—unlike equities and bonds they don't generate cash flows during the holding period; and (2) the Family Inc. portfolio is already reasonably well positioned to combat inflation because after-tax labor, after-tax Social Security benefits, equities, and the family's real estate holdings are all likely to grow with inflation over the long term. Furthermore, the long-term historical returns for commodities such as gold are just not that compelling. As we'll see in Chapter 10, after inflation, gold's long-term compounded annual return has been approximately 0.7 percent.

If you become wealthy enough that labor assets, Social Security, and family real estate become an insignificant component of total Family Inc. Net Worth, incremental exposure to commodities can provide diversification and noncorrelation benefits. Even then, if you want additional commodity exposure, I recommend owning equities of commodity-oriented businesses rather than the commodity itself. These businesses are highly correlated with the underlying commodities and therefore provide a good hedge against inflation, but in addition to the opportunity for commodity appreciation, they can provide cash through dividends along the way. If you want inflation protection from gold, buy gold mining stock, not gold itself.

Or don't. Even if you feel you need the inflation protection associated with commodities, I recommend avoiding gold. I prefer other highly liquid commodities that are traded in dollars just like gold, but unlike gold, possess real underlying intrinsic value beyond being a form of currency. Examples include oil, natural gas, copper, or silver.

Real estate. Real estate represents a significant component of most Family Inc. portfolios because many families own their primary residence. Yet while families include homes in their net worth statements, they usually ignore them when they come to think about allocating their assets. Your home represents a substantial asset within your portfolio, but that doesn't necessarily make it an attractive investment. Purchasing real estate, both primary and vacation homes, should be viewed as both an investment and a consumption decision. While many investments in real estate have historically performed well, they are likely to do poorly in the future for the following reasons. Owning real estate comes with a variety of hidden costs such as maintenance, taxes, lawn care, furnishings, and utilities. Primary residences and vacation homes generate little income but often come with substantial carrying costs such as mortgage payments and property taxes. Real estate is illiquid. It often takes several months to sell, and broker and transfer fees can drain away as much as 7 percent to 8 percent of the total asset value.

Over the long run, real estate is likely to appreciate at a rate close to the rate of inflation. In the past several decades, real estate investors in the United States and globally benefited from reductions in interest rates, abnormally high demand from baby boomers, innovation in financing products that dramatically increased the pool of potential buyers, and increased government subsidies through tax deductions and financing support from intermediaries such as Freddie Mac and Fannie Mae. These dynamics are unlikely to repeat themselves anytime soon. Even in this positive environment, house prices increased only approximately 2 percent per year after inflation from 1975 to 2005. Over a longer period (1890–2000) there was little real house price appreciation in the United States. Within a reasonable range of assumptions for inflation and appreciation, real estate returns are likely to be less attractive than equity returns, with less liquidity, more hidden costs, more work, and greater risk of loss.

■ Key Conclusions

Diversification and the benefits of owning uncorrelated assets are core tenets of a sound investment strategy. The benefits of diversification are one of the few "free lunches" in investing—you get the benefits of less volatility without compromising expected gains.

Consensus asset-allocation models promoted by most investment advisers are inadequate. They fail to account for all the assets of the Family Business such as labor, Social Security benefits, and family real estate; they underestimate most families' time horizons; and they allocate funds to fixed income investments as a percentage of a portfolio rather than dollar amounts based on anticipated spending.

Employing the principles of an asset-allocation model within the Family Inc. framework results in significantly greater equity exposure and significantly less exposure to bonds and real estate than the conventional models call for.

Sorry, Stan.

CHAPTER 9

Define the Right Goals for Your Asset Management Business

When discussing their investment experiences, many people gravitate to their "home runs" or the "quick flips" in which they doubled their money in a few months. While these stories can be entertaining, they are immaterial in the broader context of your portfolio performance goals. The relevant measure of your asset management business is the *long-term return on your portfolio after fees, taxes, and inflation*, with *return* defined as the internal rate of return, or IRR. This metric highlights the components of investment returns that must be actively managed, including:

- *Gross return*. The dominant factor driving IRR is gross return—your gains or losses versus the cumulative cash flows you have invested. The factors that influence gross return include (a) asset-class composition—are you invested in fixed income securities or equities?;

(b) performance within the asset class—how did your specific investments or your selected manager perform in relation to the rest of the asset class?*; and (c) invested position—how much of your assets have you actively invested? I define investments as assets that carry risk, either in the form of credit or capital risk (the likelihood of loss) or duration risk (the likelihood that conditions will change over time, as with a 30-year Treasury bond or a stock). Being uninvested doesn't necessarily imply zero return. Bank accounts that are insured up to FDIC limits, T-bills with less than 90-day maturities, and money market funds all count as uninvested for me—they carry practically no credit or duration risk and thus have minimal returns. By this definition, your invested position can range from zero percent to 100 percent of total available investment assets, or even 150 percent through margin borrowing. In other words, if you have $100 in your portfolio, you could choose to invest anywhere from zero to $150.

- *Inflation.* While you can't influence this variable, it erodes the purchasing power of your assets and drags down your real returns, and so must be considered as you define your investment objectives. Allowing for inflation will affect not only your investment strategy, but also the magnitude of the amounts you will require to sustain your family's chosen way of life.

- *Tax leakage.* Taxes can have a meaningful influence on portfolio performance. Various investment strategies can have significantly different implications. Depending on your income and home state, long-term gains can be taxed as much as 30 percent and short-term gains (on investments held less than 12 months), in the 50 percent range. These higher rates apply to interest on fixed income investments and to short-term capital gains on equities. According to a Vanguard study comparing investment strategies, actively managed mutual funds resulted in median annual tax costs of 1.9 percent of the assets invested while index funds, which trade securities less often and therefore incur fewer taxable gains, resulted in median annual tax costs of 1.07 percent—a difference of $830 a year on a $100,000 investment. ETFs (exchange-traded funds) composed of stocks are even more tax efficient because their only significant taxable income comes from dividends, not selling shares to

*The difference between an individual security's, or manager's, performance and the average performance, adjusted for the riskiness of the holding, is known on Wall Street as *alpha*.

satisfy redemptions. Investment strategies and their tax consequences matter!

- *Fee leakage.* Management fees, incentive fees, and operating expenses of investment products are a further drag on performance. They can take multiple forms. For example, actively managed mutual funds often burden investors with annual management fees and operating expenses that range from 0.5 to 1.5 percent (50 to 150 basis points) of managed assets, while index funds tend to be less expensive, ranging from 5 to 80 basis points.

Funds investing in lower risk, more liquid securities such as government bonds, corporate bonds, and large-capitalization U.S. stocks charge the least, and those specializing in emerging international markets such as Brazil, Russia, India, and China charge the most. Actively managed funds other than mutual funds, such as hedge funds and private equity funds, often charge an incentive fee—usually 20 percent of the gain above a minimum return threshold—in addition to an annual management fee, often 2 percent.

While these percentage numbers—0.5 to 2.0 percent of total assets under management—may not seem that significant at first, they can represent a powerful drag on performance when viewed as a percentage of appreciation rather than of total assets under management. For example, the real long-term appreciation of U.S. stocks over the past 200-plus years has averaged about 6.5 percent, so 2 percent in fees and expenses would have taken almost one-third of those gains.

■ Where the Money Disappears

Figure 9.1 shows the cumulative impact of tax, expense, and inflation leakage over a 30-year period by comparing various gross returns, inflation-adjusted (real) returns, and inflation-adjusted after-fee returns (IRRs) for both low- and high-cost strategies. The low-cost strategy shown assumes annual management and operating expenses of 0.5 percent and portfolio turnover of 20 percent per year that qualifies for long-term capital gains treatment. The high-cost results are based on annual management and operating expenses of 2 percent and portfolio turnover of 100 percent per year, of which 50 percent qualifies as long-term capital gains and 50 percent is taxed as short-term income. (Dividends and interest are excluded from this comparison because rates and taxes differ greatly among investors. Taxes on any dividends and interest received would further lower the net returns.)

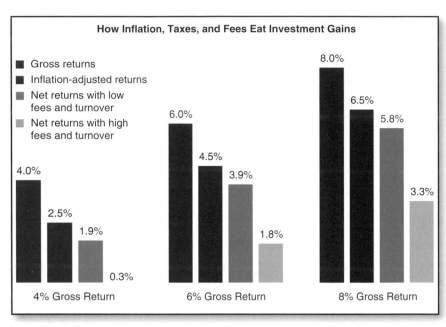

FIGURE 9.1 Average Annual Returns (IRRs) over 30 Years Based on Three Different Gross Returns

As shown, these sources of leakage degrade your real purchasing power between about 25 and 90 percent relative to the gross return. The lower the expected gross return, the higher the percentage of leakage and the more punitive the impact.

The damage becomes even more apparent when viewed in dollar terms. Figure 9.2 shows how one dollar grows over 30 years based on the same gross, inflation-adjusted, and real net return scenarios.

When the leakage from inflation, fees, and taxes is compounded over a long period, the impact is enormous. Figure 9.2's 6 percent scenario, for example, shows it reduces the gross appreciation by 45 percent even with a low-cost strategy and 70 percent with a high-cost strategy.

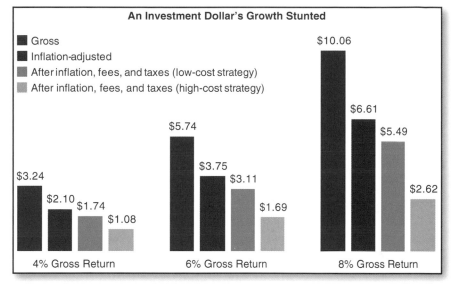

FIGURE 9.2 Value after 30 Years Based on Three Different Gross Returns

■ Key Conclusions

The future purchasing power of your assets is net of inflation, taxes, and fees. Those sources of leakage represent a significant percentage of your gross returns and materially degrade future purchasing power.

Maximizing real, after-tax, after-fee returns by minimizing the sources of this leakage must therefore be a core tenet of your family asset management business.

CHAPTER 10

Use History to Make Reasonable Investment Assumptions

As Warren Buffett has observed, if past investment performance could predict future performance, the Forbes 400 would be composed of librarians. Still, reviewing historical returns, some over very long periods, can provide useful guidance about the relative attractiveness of each major asset class and some reasonable expectations about future performance. In this chapter, we analyze historical asset class returns and volatility to explore the implications for your Family Inc. investment strategy.

Much of my thinking on this topic has been influenced not only by my personal investing experiences, but also by the works of Jeremy Siegel and David Swensen, two of today's leading writers on investment theory. For more information on the data and theoretical underpinnings supporting some of the conclusions regarding asset class behavior, I recommend their writings. This book was written for the practitioner—the Family CFO— and is meant to address what you should do. Jeremy and David provide additional insight regarding *why* these recommendations are well founded.

■ Long-Term Investment Returns

Figure 10.1 demonstrates that while equities are significantly more volatile than government bonds and T-bills, they almost invariably perform significantly better over long periods.

This comparison and its supporting data provide a variety of valuable insights regarding the relative attractiveness of equities:

■ Adjusted for inflation over the centuries, the compound annual total return for stocks (dividends plus capital gains) has outperformed long-term government bonds by 3 percentage points. Equities outperformed bonds not only for the entire 200-year-plus period, but also in every major economic period analyzed since World War II.

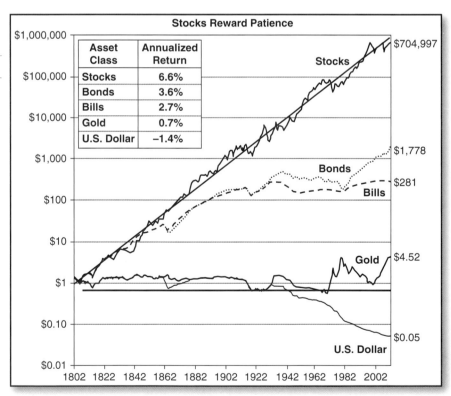

FIGURE 10.1 Inflation-Adjusted Growth of a $1 U.S. Investment, 1802–2012
Source: Jeremy J. Siegel, *Stocks for the Long Run*, 5th ed. (New York: McGraw-Hill, 2014), 82.

- Real compound annual total return for equities outperformed *short*-term government bills by approximately 4 percentage points over the total period analyzed and exceeded returns of short-term government bonds in every sub-period analyzed except for 1966–1981, when equities provided real compound annual returns of –0.4 percent and short-term government bonds provided real compound annual returns of –0.2 percent.

- Equities' superior long-term returns are accompanied by much greater annual price volatility. Furthermore, since the volatility of government bonds is driven by changes in the underlying interest rate, even these lesser fluctuations can be eliminated through the purchase of Treasury Inflation Protected Securities (TIPS). But the investor pays a significant premium for this reduced volatility. In 2016, 10-year TIPS yielded 0.6 percent—a 70 percent discount from the 2 percent yield of the equivalent 10-year U.S. government bond. While it's not the primary focus of this comparison, note that real returns for equities have also dramatically outperformed the average real return for gold, by 5.9 percentage points a year from 1802 to 2012.

It's safe to say that over the long term, the market continues to provide a real risk premium for equities over fixed income. Over the past 150 years, history records exactly one 30-year period during which equities underperformed fixed income securities.* Furthermore, the risk premium that equity investors collect in the form of improved returns is not simply an American phenomenon. With a few anomalies recorded in specific countries and periods (for example, Japan from 1990 to 2015), this equity risk premium has existed in all major developed and emerging-market economies for more than a century. One study of global returns found that the average annual real returns of 19 countries from 1900 to 2012 were 4.6 percent and the average world equity premium over bonds was 3.7 percent, versus 3 percent in the United States. With an appropriately long time horizon and a globally diversified equity portfolio, investors can count on benefiting from this premium.

---

*This occurred during the 30 years that ended in 2011, when continually declining interest rates lifted fixed income dramatically above its long-term average performance, not because equities languished.

■ Living with Volatility

Clearly, investors are handsomely compensated for owning equities, but this comes with substantially more short-term volatility. One study analyzed the range of annual gains and losses over 80 years of different possible portfolio mixes, from zero percent stocks and 100 percent bonds to 100 percent stocks and zero percent bonds. Annual returns for the all-stock portfolio have ranged from approximately +40 percent to –40 percent. These extreme occurrences, however, are rare. Over the 80 years analyzed, yearly losses in excess of 10 percent occurred 10 times (or 13 percent of the time) with an average loss in those 10 years of about 12 percent. While no one enjoys a year of losses, these losses were more than recovered: Stocks posted gains in 70 percent of the years studied.

Asset price volatility is a real risk that investors must recognize as they manage their assets, but the risk is generally overstated. Without doubt, equities show greater annual price swings than bonds and T-bills. But for most of us, this measure is largely academic because the expected duration of our investments is generally very long, even for most families near or in retirement. The three charts that make up Figure 10.2 show how equities' volatility decreases dramatically as the years go by.

The volatility of one-year returns is dramatically higher than that of returns for five years, which, in turn, are higher than for 25 years. In other words, as your time horizon stretches, your expected annualized long-term return remains constant, but the volatility you must endure to achieve it diminishes. Indeed, as Figure 10.3 shows, equities' gradual decline of volatility has made them *less* risky than bonds or T-bills over 30 years.

Given the frequency of outperformance and the magnitude of the difference in returns—equities provided approximately twice the real return of fixed income—the case for equities is increasingly compelling the longer the expected holding period.

While investors are generally compensated over time for accepting annual volatility, it is still a significant risk that must be actively managed. Specifically, asset price volatility affects how much risk Family CFOs can assume in the rest of their asset-management business through decisions like employing leverage in the portfolio, incurring long-term fixed debt such as a mortgage, and determining the desired amount of liquid investments to manage the risk of unemployment.

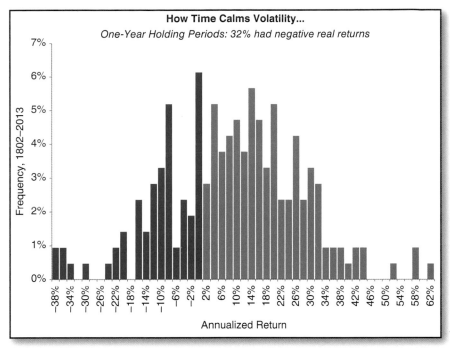

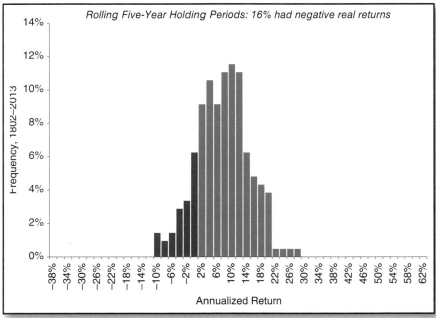

FIGURE 10.2 Change in Returns Over Various Five-Year Periods
Source: Data from jeremysiegel.com.

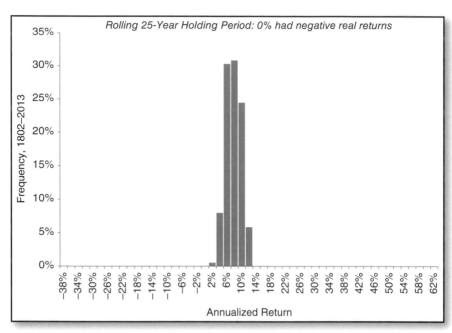

FIGURE 10.2 *Continued*

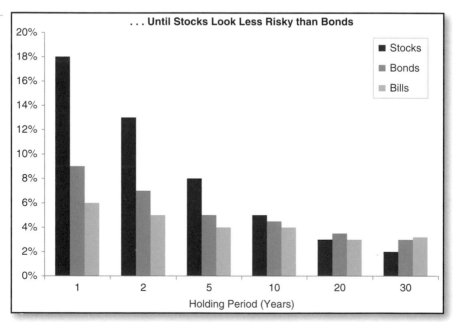

FIGURE 10.3 Average Annual Volatility of After-Inflation Returns
Source: Jeremy J. Siegel, *The Future for Investors: Why the Tried and the True Triumph Over the Bold and the New* (New York: Random House, 2005), 174.

Should You Borrow?

If equities consistently beat fixed income by such a large margin with relatively low long-term volatility, is it prudent to borrow money, usually by margin loans from a broker, to get additional exposure to equities? Historical return analysis and well regarded academics such as Jeremy Siegel actually recommend such a strategy. Many hedge funds and alternative asset managers such as leveraged buyout funds also employ leverage—borrowing—to enhance returns. For investors with a high tolerance for risk and with expected duration, or time horizon, in excess of 10 years, Siegel recommends employing leverage ranging from approximately 10 to 40 percent of the portfolio, which provides an equity allocation ranging from 110 to 140 percent of the amount invested. While I agree with Siegel's premise—prudent leverage can be good—I recommend caution in applying it to your family business, which may already employ leverage for purchasing assets such as real estate and cars. We explore this subject in greater detail in Section IV, but suffice it to say here that leverage can be a prudent way to enhance returns for investors with adequate liquidity and a long time horizon.

How Do Taxes Affect the Case for Equities?

The case for equities gets even better when you consider the tax implications. Current tax policy imposes federal income tax rates as high as 39.6 percent on interest and short-term capital gains—and the total bite can exceed

Period	STOCKS Tax Brackets				BONDS Tax Brackets			
	$0	$50K	$150K	Max	$0	$50K	$150K	Max
1871–2012	6.5%	5.2%	4.7°%	4.1%	3.0%	2.0%	1.7%	1.2%
1982–2012	7.8%	5.5%	5.3°%	5.3%	7.6%	4.8%	4.4%	4.3%

Period	T-BILLS Tax Brackets				MUNI BONDS	GOLD	CPI
	$0	$50K	$150K	Max			
1871–2012	1.6%	0.8%	0.1%	− 0.4%	2.2%	1.0%	2.0%
1982–2012	1.6%	0.1%	−1.0%	−1.7%	3.4%	1.8%	2.9%

FIGURE 10.4 The Tax Effect: After-Tax Real Asset Returns, 1871–2012: Compound Annual Rates of Return
Source: Jeremy J. Siegel, *Stocks for the Long Run*, 5th ed. (New York: McGraw-Hill, 2014), 136.

50 percent depending on your state income tax rate. Capital gains tax rates—20 to 30 percent, depending on your income—apply to long-term capital gains and most dividends. As Figure 10.4 shows, when including taxes at the maximum rates, real after-tax returns suffer for both equities and fixed income, but Uncle Sam's take is substantially higher for fixed income.

■ Theory versus Real World Application

We have made a pretty compelling case for the merits of equity ownership over fixed income in increasing and preserving after-tax purchasing power. Yet there is still real resistance among investors to deploying this strategy. I have had this discussion on numerous occasions with my father, who still has way more fixed income exposure than I think is warranted. When I cite the long list of academic studies and theory to support my conclusion, his consistent retort has been, "You can't eat theory."

The great news for Dad and all investors is that the real-world application of this strategy of maximizing equity exposure over a lifetime actually works even better than theory would suggest. This happens because of the timing of cash flows that occur over a lifetime as people save for the first 40 or 50 years of their lives and then deplete savings for the next 20 or 30 years. Here's why:

Returns are better than expected. The long-term returns presented earlier in this chapter are calculated by assuming only two transactions: an investment in 1802 that generates dividends that are reinvested along the way and a sale in 2012. In your personal situation, however, your investments from your twenties until your sixties are likely to occur several times a year and represent over 100 different entry points over four decades of saving. Practically, this is the same as employing dollar cost averaging whereby your investment dollars buy more when market values are depressed and less when they're high. Similarly, in real life retirement, you don't liquidate your portfolio in any one year, but rather over many years. This dollar cost averaging results in average annual real returns of 7.1 percent over a 60-year investment period—half a percentage point better than the annualized return over the entire period from 1802 to 2012.

Figure 10.5 demonstrates how well equities work in this kind of real life scenario. In this case, a person invests $10,000 a year for 40 years, from ages 25 to 65, then, each year for the next 19 years, takes out 5 percent of the amount that was in the portfolio at age 65, with a final distribution of the remaining value at age 85. The three lines on the chart show, for each year

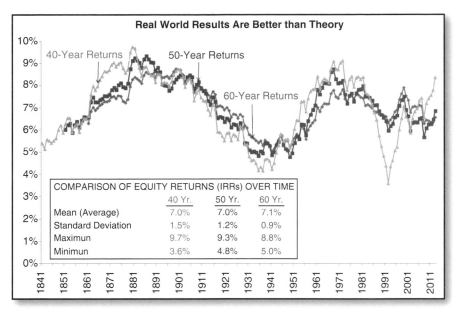

FIGURE 10.5 Real Lifetime Returns

since 1841, the average annual return that investor would have realized after following that program for 40, 50, and 60 years, respectively.*

Volatility is less than expected. As shown, average compounded real equity returns were close to 7 percent for 40-, 50-, and 60-year programs. Volatility (measured as standard deviation) for the 60-year program, for example, was 0.9 percent. This means there is a 68.2 percent chance your return will be between 6.2 and 8.0 percent and a 95 percent chance your returns will be within 5.3 and 8.9 percent. In no instance over any 60-year period was the compounded annual real return less than 5 percent.

Volatility decreases as the holding period increases. The periodic buying and selling over the course of the family life cycle further dampens volatility compared to results from a specific period with one entry point and one exit point. Taxes will also mitigate volatility: When your investments gain, you share some with Uncle Sam; when your investments lose, you get to net these losses against other present or future gains. This has a dampening effect on volatility.

---

* These circumstances were applied to actual inflation-adjusted equity returns for successive 40-, 50-, and 60-year periods ended from 1841 to 2013. Taxes were not included because tax policy changes and rates for individual circumstances cause huge variance, but it can be said that in all cases taxes are more punitive for fixed income investors than equity investors.

■ When Markets Gyrate, Think Like a Business Owner

In spite of the logic and historical results that support high equity exposure, many people just can't get their heads around the risk. The possibility of seeing the portfolio drop by as much as 40 percent in a year is just too much to bear. If you're among those who have a hard time stomaching this short-term volatility, I encourage you to forget about the day-to-day and year-to-year movements of the markets and think and act like a business owner rather than a speculator. Most successful business owners have a long-term focus—they measure success not by quarters or years, but by decades. These owners measure performance not by stock price but by profit and cash flow growth. They don't focus on the price that some investor would pay for their business today because this is their livelihood and they intend to own it for their working lifetime. They instead take comfort in knowing that in every year the business generates positive cash flow, they have reduced their risk and built their net worth. They know if they build a business that consistently increases profits and cash flow while providing a valuable service to its customers, it will be a valuable asset when it comes time to sell.

As investors, we are well served to think like that business owner. When you buy an ETF representing the S&P 500, you are not just buying paper that moves with the whims of the market. You are buying a small share of every company in the index—iconic brands like Apple, Microsoft, ExxonMobil, J&J, GE, Wells Fargo, Berkshire Hathaway, AT&T, Pfizer, Amazon, Facebook, Google, P&G, Walt Disney, Coca-Cola, Home Depot, Intel, Walmart, McDonald's, and Boeing. These companies have solid brands, good management, and strong balance sheets, and serve a broad range of industries and customers with valued products or services. As an investor in the S&P 500, you are like the owner of a good individual company except your business is more diversified and less likely to underperform over the long term.

As we saw when assessing prospective employers in Chapter 5, over time a company's growth and earnings determine an investor's gains. The same is true for the group of companies represented by an index. The S&P 500 stock index has experienced numerous years in negative territory, with annual losses approaching 45 percent. In spite of all this price volatility, the companies that together make up the index have never had an unprofitable year since the index was established in the 1870s. Furthermore, there has never been a year when the S&P didn't pay a dividend. Almost 150 years of history and not one year of losses or forgone payments to equity holders! Have earnings and dividends decreased or increased dramatically from year to year with the economy? You bet! But a business owner knows that the company's long-term value isn't determined by a bad year (and neither are your investments), but rather decades of performance and projected cash flows. With that time horizon in mind, the S&P business looks great.

The S&P 500's real compound earnings growth was approximately 1.8 percent annually from 1870 through 2014. Real earnings growth over a decade was positive 70 percent of the time, and when there was a decrease in earnings, it was relatively small. The largest decrease in real earnings was approximately 15 percent over a decade (1.5 percent per year on average). That happened during the 1921–1930 boom and bust that ushered in the Great Depression. Yet even in those economic dark times, the S&P business generated positive earnings and cash flows, and paid dividends to owners. S&P 500 dividend growth averaged 1.5 percent annually from 1870 through 2014 with the largest drop in real dividends—averaging a little less than 1 percent a year—occurring in the 1970s. In other words, while stock prices may be volatile, the underlying long-term cash flow and dividend growth of the S&P 500 have been very resilient.

As an investor, it is easy to get caught up in the ups and downs of the markets and to panic when prices decline. But as an owner, you can take great comfort that your S&P business will surely make a profit and pay a dividend this year as it has every other year. Because the earnings and dividends over a reasonably long period will also be stable and probably growing, you have the simple luxury of doing nothing when markets gyrate. Just because the market may offer you less right now than it was willing to offer last year doesn't mean that your asset management business is worth any less to you. It just means that you will need to own your business a bit longer and continue to benefit from the earnings and dividend growth until you find an attractive buyer.

■ Combining History with Today's Environment

Given this extensive history of long-term real global returns of approximately 5.5 percent and acknowledging that individuals pay dramatically different fees and taxes, most of the analysis in this book conveniently assumes 5 percent real returns after taxes and fees for our sample family. That offers a reasonable starting point, indicating what an investor actually would have achieved over the past 200–plus years with a portfolio weighted according to global market capitalizations. But such analysis may not be helpful in developing an accurate estimate of future returns. Neither I nor anyone else can forecast future returns precisely. The data regarding historical returns and volatility do, however, allow us to predict a range of real returns with some expectation of success. For example, while I have little confidence that the next 30 years will deliver real global returns as high as 5.5 percent, history allows us to predict that real global returns will be between 3.5 and 7.5 percent (plus or minus one standard deviation around the average) with a 68.2 percent expectation of success, and that returns will be greater than 3.5 percent with an 84 percent expectation of success.

While those calculations are statistically sound, the range in wealth creation resulting from long-term returns between 3.5 and 7.5 percent is unacceptably large for planning purposes. As always, there are threats and opportunities that make this range so large. The headwinds facing the markets today are numerous and significant: high valuations, lower growth prospects due to unsustainable government deficits and high sovereign debt levels, the prospect of ongoing global conflict, and more. On the other hand, significant opportunities for continued global economic growth include continued economic expansion in emerging markets, long-term prospects for low interest rates and inflation, and continued commitment to market-based economies and pro-growth government policies. Innovations in business, technology, and energy will continue to promote global growth.

As we evaluate the impact of these risks and opportunities on future returns, it's helpful to deconstruct the sources of the returns for equities— free cash flows to equity, growth in earnings, and the change in price that someone is willing to pay for a dollar of earnings (P/E ratio).

- Free cash flow to equity* can be used to pay investors in two ways: (a) paid as dividends to equity holders as compensation for holding the stock during the period, and (b) to repurchase outstanding shares. Dividends for the S&P 500 recently represented a yield of 2.25 percent versus a historical average of approximately 4.4 percent. Share repurchases generally increase earnings per share, which is a second source of value.

- Real annual growth in earnings per share for the S&P 500 has been approximately 1.8 percent over the past 150 years and is generally correlated with long-term growth in the economy.

---

*Free cash flow to equity is a metric of how much cash can be paid to the equity shareholders after all cash expenses, taxes, reinvestments, and net borrowings.

- The P/E ratio of the S&P 500 has recently been approximately 20 times annual earnings, higher than the 150-year average of about 15.5. While high relative to historical norms, the current P/E of 20 can in part be justified by the ultra-low interest rate environment and, relative to history, better financial information, greater liquidity, lower transaction costs, and favorable tax treatment for capital income over interest income.

Of these factors, I believe current market valuations and the corresponding lower dividend yields represent the largest risk to investors. While returns will be driven predominantly by dividends and earnings growth in the long term, valuation compression—lower P/Es—is likely to result in a modest drag on future returns. For these reasons, it's logical to assume a long-term real return of 4 to 5 percent a year for equities, which is comfortably within the range predicted by our historic analysis. As markets evolve, this is an area where a good financial adviser should be able to help you bridge historical results to reasonable forecasts adjusted for your individual tax and fee profile.

■ Managing in a World of Dollars, Not Percentages

The historical performance presented in this chapter makes a pretty compelling argument that equities have a higher expected long-term return than other asset classes (the equity risk premium) and that the volatility of this expected internal rate of return decreases with a longer time horizon. This doesn't mean, of course, that equity owners fully escape all risks or insulate themselves from the negative impacts of bad returns. But it does give them significant predictive ability in the real world where consumption needs and financial obligations require actual purchasing power, not percentages.

Consider, for example, the difference between my father's time horizon and mine. Let's assume that global real equity returns will be 5 percent. Dad has a five-year planning horizon, which, as the history summarized in Figure 10.3 suggests, is likely to experience volatility (standard deviation) of eight percentage points around the expected return. In contrast, I have a 30-year time horizon, for which volatility has been two percentage points. Table 10.1 highlights the ranges of outcomes for Dad and me within a 95 percent probability (that is, our returns will be within the high and low ranges 95 percent of the time).

TABLE 10.1 Our Future in Percentages...

	Dad	Me
Age	80	45
Time horizon (years)	5	30
Expected real internal rate of return	5%	5%
Volatility of return (standard deviation)	8%	2%
Highest expected return	21%	9%
Lowest expected return	−11%	1%

In Table 10.1, it looks as though I have much less risk and much less upside than Dad. Dad can expect a range of annualized returns between −11 percent and +21 percent over his five-year holding period while my range of outcomes is much narrower—between +1 and +9 percent. When we examine this same scenario in dollar terms, however, the result is exactly opposite.

Because of the power of compounding over time, Table 10.2 shows that even though I have a much narrower range of outcomes as defined by annualized returns, my range of wealth outcomes is much greater than Dad's. At the end of Dad's investment period, he can expect to have between about $6,000 and $26,000, a $20,000 difference. I on the other hand can expect to have between about $13,000 and $133,000, or a range of $119,000 in possible ending wealth.

Three key points to remember from the above sections are these: (1) the volatility of returns decreases over time, (2) because of the compounding effect, the impact of these variations in returns increases with time, and (3) it's always important to translate investment results into real-world dollars to understand the practical impact on your financial planning.

TABLE 10.2 ...and in Dollars

	Dad	Me
Investment	$10,000	$10,000
Time horizon (years)	5	30
Expected end amount	$12,763	$43,219
Highest end amount	$25,937	$132,677
Lowest end amount	$5,584	$13,478
Range of expectations	$20,353	$119,198

◼ Key Conclusions

Most investment advisers incorrectly define clients' appetite for risk and its implications for asset allocation. Risk appetite is not just some amorphous concept reflecting an individual's personality—that's an investment adviser's cop-out for blaming you for your asset allocation decision if things go poorly. Your risk appetite should be based on the expected duration of your investments before you need to cash them in. Properly seen, investors with a long expected duration have a high-risk appetite while those with a short duration have a low-risk appetite.

For investors with a long expected duration who are focused on real, after-tax, after-fee purchasing power, there is no trade-off between risk and return. Equities offer greater expected returns with lower risk.

Equity prices can rise and fall dramatically from year to year, but over a long duration, the combination of lessening volatility and higher expected total return actually makes a diversified portfolio of equities less risky than bonds.

Different tax treatment for stocks and bonds makes the after-tax comparisons even more favorable to equities.

Government bonds and bills should not be viewed as attractive assets for generating investment gain or income, but rather as a source of liquidity and capital preservation over a short to medium time horizon.

Globally, bonds return about 1.5 percent a year after inflation over the long term. Adjusted for taxes, this return is closer to 1 percent for most families.

Adjusted for inflation, long-term compound returns have historically been 6.6 percent for U.S. equities before taxes and fees, and 4.6 percent for global equities. There is no reason that U.S. equities should perpetually outperform other world markets. On the contrary, reversion to the mean is more likely. Furthermore, changing global conditions make it prudent to expect somewhat lower returns. Given today's market environment, a reasonable assumption for future performance is a global real compound rate of return of 4 to 5 percent adjusted for your individual tax and fee circumstances.

We can predict with greater certainty the relative performance of stocks and bonds than we can the absolute performance. The real global premium of equity over bonds is surprisingly consistent over the long run at about 4 percentage points. You can take comfort in knowing that regardless of what the future may hold, the long-term growth in real purchasing power for equities is highly likely to exceed that of fixed income: Investors will continue to be compensated to accept the short-term volatility of equities.

CHAPTER 11

Safeguard Your Assets from the Main Risks

The historical risks and returns of various asset classes provide a valuable framework for family investment decisions. Price volatility is certainly one risk the Family CFO must consider, but it's far from the only one. As we saw in Chapter 6, the most catastrophic Family Inc. risk is the impairment of family members' labor asset (the potential value of their work) resulting from death or disability. Fortunately, this risk can be mitigated through insurance. Other major types of risk the family must contend with include impairment of financial assets, inflation, and shortfall risk.

Asset impairment occurs when the value of an investment is permanently impaired—that is, all or a substantial part of the investment is wiped out. Three common examples include bankruptcy of a privately owned business, foreclosure on a house, and personal bankruptcy. As you might surmise from these examples, impairment is most likely in privately held investments, so investors generally demand a higher rate of return to compensate them for that risk, as well as for the lack of liquidity. For most families, however, the main private investments are the primary residence or the family business—which, if managed prudently, possess relatively low risk of impairment.

Inflation represents a significant risk to family assets. It erodes future purchasing power, requiring greater net worth to support retirement. This threat is compounded because asset prices generally decline during periods of increasing inflation. Inflation is one of the most underappreciated risks because it happens slowly and is anticipated. But over the long term, inflation represents a much bigger risk to purchasing power than impairment risk or asset price volatility. Annual inflation has averaged approximately 3 percent over most of the past 100 years, and has been greater than zero more than 83 percent of the time.

Still, when measuring real returns (nominal returns minus inflation), the risk profile of various asset classes looks very different. Adjusted for inflation, stocks provided a negative return in only one decade since the 1920s while Treasuries (long-term, medium-term, and short-term) generated negative returns in about half the decades.

Figure 11.1 shows how these differences affected the returns of three kinds of investment portfolios. For example, in nominal terms (the dark blue columns) a portfolio composed entirely of Treasury bills never had a losing year, but after inflation (the light blue columns), it lost money more than a third of the time.

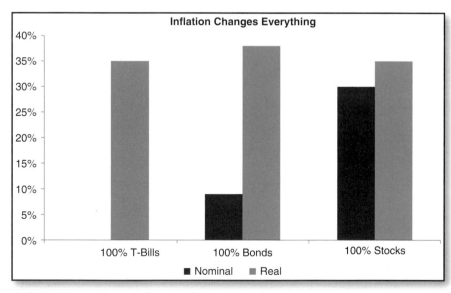

FIGURE 11.1 Percent of Years with Negative Return
Source: Vanguard Investment Counseling and Research, "Portfolio Construction for Taxable Investors," 4.

Rising inflation is highly correlated with poor market returns. Between 1926 and 2008, average real returns for stocks, government bonds, and Treasury bills were negative in any year that inflation increased by more than 1.5 percent and positive on average in years when inflation rose less than 1.5 percent. Furthermore, when inflation slowed, average real returns of stocks and government bonds exceeded their long-term averages. In a world in which cause and effect are often difficult to establish, the negative impact of inflation is pretty clear and perhaps the single most relevant factor in determining real asset returns.

Since inflation shatters real returns for all major asset classes, a long-term investor's best choice, really, is to pursue the least bad alternative—equities. Inflation weakens equity prices, too, but over time, equities are likely to retain value from inflated profits and cash flows, and when inflation subsides, equity valuations rebound as well. Equities not only have the highest expected return, but also remain the best long-term hedge against inflation.

Shortfall risk measures the likelihood that an individual or an organization will not have enough assets to fund a specified liability. This concept is frequently employed by pension and endowment managers to assess how likely they are to meet their commitments. For Family Inc., shortfall risk (also referred to as *longevity risk*) measures the probability that a family or individual will outlive their accumulated financial resources. This risk is relatively hard to quantify and is often determined through use of a technique referred to as Monte Carlo simulation, which forecasts the probability of missing a specified objective. While subject to numerous, hard-to-predict assumptions, this is the single most important risk metric that a family should actively manage and monitor. In addition to gauging the probability of outliving your money, a shortfall analysis is an extremely valuable tool in evaluating the relative merits of various investment strategies in the context of long-term retirement planning. See Chapter 19 for a simplified example of how shortfall analysis can be employed.

■ Key Conclusions

Inflation is a bigger threat to your financial security than volatility or asset impairment, but the risk most important to protect against is shortfall—running out of money in retirement.

Unfortunately, there is really no good way to fully protect yourself from inflation but asset ownership in the form of stocks, real estate, or commodities is the best long-term hedge.

To minimize the chances of big losses, nonprofessional investors should steer clear of private alternative assets such as venture capital and private equity, and avoid investments in individual securities that aren't part of a broadly diversified investment plan. No index ever went to zero.

CHAPTER 12

Not All Debt Is Bad! Use Debt to Purchase Assets and Maximize Your Liquidity

Debt can play an important role in Family Inc., both as an investment and as a source of funding. The general perception is that for an investor, debt is a good, safe investment—bonds, notes, and CDs, the debt of corporations, governments, and banks—while for a borrower, debt is bad. Let's explore these two assumptions.

■ Debt or Fixed Income as an Investment

As part of your portfolio, fixed income securities possess two valuable attributes: preservation of value and ease of liquidation (selling for cash). The major categories of fixed income securities include Treasury bonds and bills, municipal bonds, and corporate bonds (investment grade and non-investment grade). Their possible roles in your portfolio differ.

Treasury securities. As seen in Chapter 10, the inflation-adjusted long-term return since 1871 is approximately 3.0 percent on government bonds and 1.6 percent on short-term government securities. The difference (1.4 percentage points a year) represents the yield investors require to be compensated for the additional time their money is at risk in longer-term bonds. After taxes, these returns drop to 1.2 percent and –0.4 percent, respectively.

Municipal bonds generally have slightly lower nominal returns than Treasuries, but because the interest they pay is nontaxable, their after-tax returns are marginally higher than Treasuries to reflect the incremental risk associated with default (the failure of the issuing municipality to pay interest or principal on time).

Corporate bonds come in a variety of forms but are fundamentally similar to government debt obligations, except that they offer higher returns to compensate for the higher default risk. These securities cover a broad spectrum of credit quality and consequently of yields. High-quality issuers offer yields only marginally higher than Treasuries, while the so-called junk bonds of poor-quality issuers commonly offer yields in excess of 10 percent.

I recommend six principles when using debt as part of an investment portfolio:

1. Given the relatively unattractive after-tax real return of debt securities, I would include them in the portfolio only for the portion that you have set aside for contingency funds or that you anticipate liquidating in the next 36 months, perhaps for a planned major purchase. For this part of your portfolio, you are prioritizing safety (low volatility) and liquidity over appreciation.

2. Treasury bills represent the superior alternative for preserving liquidity and capital, and should play a significant part in your debt portfolio. This capital is expected to be spent relatively soon, and bonds have longer maturity dates.

3. Municipal bonds' freedom from taxation can be attractive, but the credit risk is difficult to assess. I generally view the premium over government obligations as inadequate relative to the incremental risk. If you decide to seek exposure to this part of the debt market, I would limit it to 25 percent of your debt portfolio.

4. Corporate bonds can also modestly enhance the returns of your debt portfolio. I recommend staying within the high-grade part of

this market and limiting your debt portfolio to no more than 25 percent high-grade corporate debt.

5. Avoid corporate junk bonds altogether. They are inconsistent with the needs of this part of your portfolio, which are liquidity and safety. Furthermore, if you are willing to assume junk bond–like risk, you are better off replicating that risk-reward profile through a combination of high-grade bonds and equity. Because bond interest is taxed as ordinary income, this combination is much more tax-efficient.

6. Since this part of your portfolio will support near-term consumption, your debt investments should have average weighted maturities of about three years or be purchased through a high-grade bond mutual fund that can be easily liquidated even if some of the underlying maturities are longer in duration.

■ Borrowing for Family Inc.

The perception that borrowing is bad for a family is true—partially. If debt is a vehicle to fund excess consumption—if it's used to consume items that would not have otherwise been purchased—then debt is bad. It simply results in an increased total cost for consumption. Debt can be a valuable financial planning tool, however, when it is used either to finance assets that would have otherwise been purchased with investment capital or to leverage returns on equity investments.

Using debt as an alternative to depleting investment assets. Borrowing to purchase assets such as cars and housing can be relatively attractive. For example, in 2015, auto loans were available for five years at 2 percent interest and 30-year fixed rate home mortgages were available at 4.5 percent interest for borrowers with good credit. Assuming annual inflation of 1.5 percent and tax deductibility of mortgage interest, these rates imply an effective cost of capital of approximately 0.5 percent and 1.2 percent, respectively. Assuming real long-term equity returns of approximately 5 percent per year, there is an opportunity for the family to make the spread on this cost-of-capital difference—that is, to make money the same way banks do. For example, let's assume I want to buy a small home for $100,000. I could sell $100,000 of my investments—or more if I owe capital gains tax—or I could borrow $80,000 from the bank at 4.5 percent on a 30-year fixed mortgage and take only $20,000 from my portfolio.

If I buy it with my cash, I own the house but also have no money. If I finance $80,000 and keep the money invested, I get the following scenario. At a 5 percent return, after inflation, fees, and taxes, my $80,000 of stocks generates $4,000 a year. The 4.5 percent loan interest—reduced by 1.5 percent inflation and the tax deductibility of interest (1.8 percentage points in the 40 percent combined federal and state tax bracket)—equals a real cost of borrowing of 1.2 percent, or $960 on the $80,000 borrowed. Thus, by using leverage to buy the house, I am generating an incremental return on my assets of $3,040 per year ($4,000 minus $960) in year one. This value spread should grow as my investment portfolio continues to increase at a faster rate than the cost of my loan. Over the life of the mortgage, this represents significant value, similar to creating a 30-year growing annuity with an initial annual payment of $3,040.

Using debt to leverage equity returns. Debt can also be used to magnify equity returns (and also volatility) by borrowing against your investments to buy more securities. Brokerage houses generally allow investors to borrow against their holdings up to 50 percent of market value, allowing investors to effectively achieve market exposure equal to 150 percent of their investment amount. As suggested in Chapter 10, for long-term investors who can tolerate increased volatility, debt used prudently to finance investment assets can benefit the portfolio. Intellectually, I absolutely believe in the benefits of leveraged equity investing, but this leverage must be evaluated in the context of other debts the family may have, and in my practical experiences, I have seen few people who have the nerve to stick with this approach when the markets dramatically correct—and they will!

■ Key Conclusions

Fixed interest (debt) securities are the right choice for the portion of your portfolio that you expect to liquidate within three years. Stick to a high-grade bond mutual fund or ETF containing bonds with a weighted average maturity of approximately three years.

Avoid individual bonds altogether. It's difficult to get appropriate diversification without a significant dollar investment. Active management is even less compelling for bonds than stocks given the lower expected return and smaller variation among managers' results. Additionally, individual bonds often offer less liquidity than a mutual fund or ETF.

Borrowing can be prudent if used to leverage returns on stocks or to finance assets that would otherwise be purchased by selling investments.

CHAPTER 13

Which Is Better, Active or Passive Investment Management? It Depends. . . .

105

I am exceptionally well positioned to actively manage my own investments. My day job is investing. I have a variety of subscriptions and research tools available to assist in evaluating investment prospects. I follow the markets almost every day as part of my job and as a personal interest and hobby. I have an undergraduate degree in economics and a master's degree in business administration. I read extensively on the economy, the markets, and investing.

So you might assume that I actively manage my personal investments. I don't. Most of my money is invested in passive (indexed) strategies. I choose active management only in markets or asset classes that have unique characteristics that require active management, such as hedge funds or private equity.

Let me explain. Over the past several chapters, we have determined the following:

- Our investment objective is maximizing long-term real, after-tax, after-fee returns.

- A reasonable expectation for future real equity returns is 4 to 5 percent a year adjusted for your tax and fee circumstances, with an implied long-term real premium of approximately three to four percentage points over government bonds.

- A sound investment strategy must employ an asset-allocation model that takes account of all Family Inc. assets, not just investments, to ensure diversification and minimize risk.

With these concepts in mind, we can now effectively evaluate the trade-offs of active versus passive investment strategies.

■ The Case for Passive Management

Passive investment strategies are generally employed through one of three investment vehicles: index mutual funds, ETFs (exchange-traded funds), or index futures.

Index mutual funds. Mutual funds are pooled investment vehicles managed by a fund manager. Index mutual funds simply allocate capital to mimic the return, before fees and expenses, of an underlying index, such as the S&P 500, the Dow Jones Total Stock Market Index, the Total International Composite Index, or the Barclays Capital Aggregate Bond Index. The benefit of this model relative to actively managed funds is that it requires less management and conducts trades less frequently, which results in lower fees, expenses, and tax liabilities. One important aspect of mutual funds is that they can be traded only once a day at the net asset value (NAV), which is the sum of the closing prices for the underlying assets and liabilities. When the mutual fund company receives an order to redeem shares, it may have to sell underlying securities to generate cash to redeem the shares. This forced liquidation of underlying shares causes tax leakage.

Exchange-traded funds. ETFs possess many of the characteristics of an index mutual fund, but, like a stock, they can be traded throughout the day on a stock exchange. Unlike a mutual fund, which redeems shares based on NAV, ETFs are purchased in the open market based on the price determined by supply and demand (which generally closely approximates the NAV). Because ETFs can be traded on an exchange, they are more efficient than traditional mutual funds, which are continuously issuing and redeeming shares and, to effect the transactions, buying and selling securities and maintaining liquidity positions. ETFs, therefore, tend to have even lower expenses and less tax leakage for the investor—although some issuers, such as Vanguard, now charge the same fees on the equivalent mutual funds as on ETFs. Given the liquidity, cost, and tax benefits, ETFs have grown rapidly. At the end of 2013, ETFs held assets of $1.6 trillion, while index mutual funds held approximately $1.7 trillion. (Actively managed mutual funds had $10.6 trillion, or slightly more than 76 percent of the mutual fund and ETF markets.)

ETFs are generally bought and sold through brokers in the same manner that stocks are bought and sold. Commissions can range from zero, if bought directly from some issuers, to $20 for online brokerage houses. They can add up, especially if you are investing in small amounts through a monthly automatic buying program. Still, while commissions can represent a real upfront cost, they become small over the investment lifetime of someone with a long-term buy and hold strategy.

The key advantage of ETFs over index mutual funds relates to tax efficiency—because ETFs trade as stocks. This has two implications. First, with an ETF, you realize no capital gains until you sell, though you do pay tax on ETF dividends. By contrast, index mutual funds reallocate their investments and redeem shares through selling and purchases, so even when you don't sell your shares, you can realize a modest tax liability driven by gains from this internal rebalancing and redemption activity. Second, index mutual funds can have an embedded tax drawback: an investor can potentially be buying into securities with a low tax basis. Say, for example, the mutual fund owns a lot of Microsoft stock that has been in the portfolio for decades. If the fund sells Microsoft, the new investor is allocated a taxable gain based on the original cost. In general, both of these impacts are relatively minor because index mutual funds attempt to limit trading—but in the world of compounding over many years and a focus on net real returns, basis points matter.

Also, because ETFs are viewed as stocks, they can be borrowed against on margin. Mutual funds generally cannot.

Index futures are simply a form of derivative based on the underlying index. This is a contract to either purchase or sell the index for a specified price at a future time (the delivery date, some time in the next 12 months). Index futures have low costs and include the ability to "short" an index (bet that it will go down). These investments, however, are not well suited for a long-term buy-and-hold strategy because any gains are triggered at the delivery date. This makes index futures relatively tax inefficient and generally more appropriate for tactical trading and short-term hedging.

TABLE 13.1 Comparison of Indexed Investments

	ETFs	Index Futures	Index Mutual Funds
Continuous trading	Yes	Yes	No
Can be sold short	Yes	Yes	No
Leverage	Can borrow 50 percent	Can borrow over 90 percent	None
Expense ratio	Extremely Low	None	Very or extremely low
Trading costs	Stock commission*	Futures commission	None
Dividend reinvestment	No*	No**	Yes
Tax efficiency	Extremely good	Poor	Very good

*Depends on policy of brokerage firm or issuer.

**Dividends are built in to the price.

Source: Jeremy J. Siegel, *Stocks for the Long Run*, 5th ed. (New York: McGraw-Hill, 2014), 283.

Since the mandate of Family Inc. revolves around maximizing long-term gains after taxes and fees, ETFs are the superior product for most Family Inc. planning needs, particularly if you can buy them without having to pay sales commissions. Table 13.1 shows the characteristics of the various indexed securities.

Indexing is a superior management approach for large, transparent, and relatively efficient markets such as U.S. equities, international developed-country equities, fixed income, and commodities. In these markets, it is difficult for active managers to consistently deliver superior returns in excess of their incremental costs. One study, of the 41 years from 1971 through 2012, showed that actively managed funds underperformed the benchmark Wilshire 5000 index by an average of 0.99 percentage points a year and the S&P 500 by 0.88 points. In fact, this underperformance is understated, as these returns exclude sales and redemption fees and the higher tax liability created through active management.

■ The Case for Active Management

Active management is appropriate in two specific instances. It can be helpful in higher risk, less efficient markets such as emerging-market equities (Brazil, Russia, India, China) and in alternative asset classes like private equity and hedge funds. These investments demonstrate significant variability of returns among managers, indicating inefficiency in the marketplace. In such an environment, good managers are more likely to consistently exceed the asset class benchmark and therefore can justify higher costs to deliver this outperformance (referred to as *alpha*). Median returns for alternative assets such as buyouts and venture capital are not necessarily higher than those from efficient markets such as U.S. equities, but the distribution of returns (perhaps the best indicator of market inefficiency) is six to nine times greater than for U.S. equities. For an investor who is capable of picking superior managers in these inefficient markets, the opportunity for alpha or outperformance is significant. One extended study found that first-quartile managers outperformed third-quartile managers by as little as 1.2 percentage points annually in U.S. fixed income and 2.5 points in U.S. equities—but by 13 points in leveraged buyouts and 21.2 points in venture capital. Given this dispersion, it can be hard for active managers in efficient markets to justify their cost, while a top-quartile manager in an inefficient asset class such as private equity is likely to pay for him- or herself several times over.

It should be noted that while emerging markets such as China and India demonstrate many of the characteristics that create inefficiency and the opportunity to achieve consistent excess returns, numerous hurdles to achieving these superior returns include higher trading costs, lack of liquidity and foreign ownership restrictions, all of which can hamper an active manager's ability to exploit these inefficient markets. Assuming you have the resources to effectively select good managers for these markets, I still advocate active management given the dispersion of manager returns.

While the data for actively managed emerging-market public equities are mixed, the case for private equities is much more compelling. Figure 13.1 demonstrates the significant variability among private equity managers, which can lead to outsize returns relative to risk—sustainable alpha—for good managers. Within the private equity category, venture capitalists fund an entrepreneur's start-up or early-stage business plan. Successful examples include Google and Facebook. Late-stage buyout firms purchase mature, profitable, proven businesses, usually with a significant amount of borrowing to improve returns on equity. Examples include KKR or Blackstone buying mature businesses like Dunkin' Donuts, J. Crew, and Dell Computer. Both venture capital and late-stage buyouts are high-risk, illiquid asset classes, but they derive their risk in different ways—venture through business risk, buyouts through financial leverage.

As Figure 13.1 suggests, both venture capital and buyouts exhibit large differences in performance among active managers, creating an opportunity for good managers to deliver value well in excess of their fees and expenses.

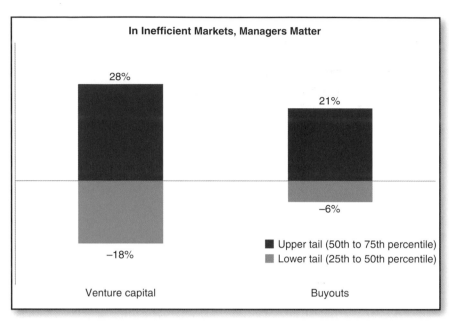

FIGURE 13.1 Annual Dispersion of Private Equity Returns, June 1988 to June 2009
Source: Vanguard Investment Counseling and Research, "Evaluating Private Equity," 8. The chart is restricted to second- and third-quartile managers to avoid distortion by outliers.

While both these private equity asset classes can be attractive, late-stage buyouts represent the more compelling risk-adjusted profile. Venture capital has demonstrated attractive long-term returns, but these seem to be biased toward the excessive returns associated with unpredictable periods of innovation such as the Internet boom of the late 1990 s. Without these outlier returns, the performance has not been as compelling, and disruptive innovations of this magnitude are infrequent as well as unpredictable. Furthermore, VC firms' returns are driven by a limited number of huge successes. It can be hard to determine if the fund manager delivered these returns through skill or luck. By contrast, exceptional buyout returns are generally driven by numerous successes and few failures, making attribution of returns easier. Lastly, buyouts have delivered better risk-adjusted returns than venture capital, as measured by the Sharpe ratio.* These are all reasons that in my own professional life I've chosen to focus on buyouts.

---

*The Sharpe ratio—calculated by subtracting the risk-free Treasury bond rate from the portfolio returns and dividing by the portfolio volatility (standard deviation)—is a simple way to communicate how much risk the investor assumed to achieve the return. We all want more return with as little risk as possible. Therefore, a high Sharpe ratio is good: It means higher returns were achieved without assuming commensurate risk.

The second area in which active management is appropriate is in asset classes showing low correlations with the broader securities markets. Examples are merger arbitrage, hedge funds, and turnaround strategies, which offer similar risk-reward attributes with low correlation to the overall portfolio. Adding these strategies can provide similar expected returns but with lower overall portfolio volatility.

◼ Key Conclusions

Passive management (indexing) is appropriate for investments in large, liquid, commoditized markets that include cash equivalents, commodities, and both debt and equity investments in efficient, mature economies like the United States, Western Europe, and Japan. Active management can be rewarding in other markets.

This bifurcation of active and passive management strategies makes common sense. Mature markets offer significant liquidity and transparency of information. These characteristics allow careful investors to forecast, estimate, understand, and price the risk, which ultimately drives down returns and dispersion of performance among managers. In such a competitive environment, it is much more difficult for any investor to consistently outperform, and therefore excess fees and taxes associated with active management are unjustified.

Emerging markets and private equity demonstrate just the opposite characteristics—illiquidity, poor transparency, and relatively sparse information. These attributes make it harder to effectively underwrite risk, so there is opportunity for skilled managers to consistently outperform the benchmarks and justify their fees. Identifying effective managers in advance, however, is challenging.

For most of the investments of Family Inc., ETFs are the preferred vehicles. They tend to be a little more tax efficient than the comparable index mutual funds.

CHAPTER 14

Use Indexing for Your Low-Cost Investment Portfolio

113

It is beyond the scope of this book to recommend specific ETFs (exchange-traded funds) or index mutual funds. Let's explore, however, the world stock markets that represent most of the equity exposure a family should desire, regardless of the branded investment product.

Figure 14.1 shows the composition of the world's stock market capitalization by region. U.S. stocks now account for half the $60 trillion value of world stocks while developed countries outside the United States make up approximately 38 percent, and emerging markets represent the remaining 12 percent. Numerous ETFs and index funds provide desired exposure to the global market at an attractive annual cost of approximately 0.3 percent. However, to constrain costs even more, I recommend dividing the developed-markets index into a U.S. index (as low as 0.05 percent annual cost) and an international index that excludes the United States (as low as 0.14 percent).

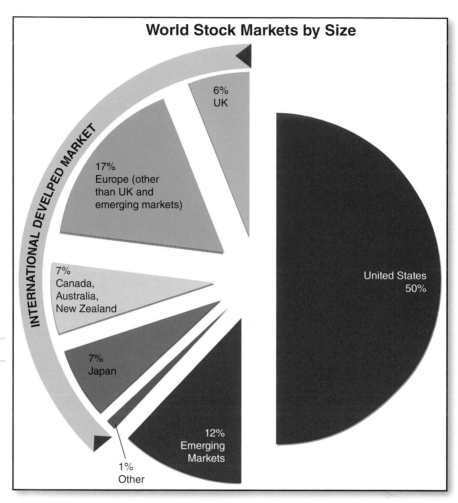

FIGURE 14.1 Weighted Capitalization of World Stock Markets
Source: MSCI ACWI Index, October 2014.

International Allocation

Analysts debate whether it's best to allocate your global equity investments according to countries' market capitalization, as charted in Figure 14.1, or country GDPs. Most indexes are based on country market capitalization, which I think understates the role of emerging markets such as China and India that have relatively large national GDPs but underdeveloped public markets. Between 1980 and 2010, the economies of emerging-market countries grew almost twice as fast as the capitalization of their stock markets.

The global nature of commerce and the dominance of multinational corporations, however, ensures that even when relying on indexes weighted by market capitalization, investors are getting significant exposure to emerging economies. Multinationals represent approximately 44 percent of total world market capitalization and, on average, derive 64 percent of their revenues from markets outside their home countries. Apple, for example, which represents 3.6 percent of the S&P 500's market value, generates 61 percent of its sales outside the United States. Almost 40 percent of all U.S. corporate earnings are now derived overseas, about double the proportion of 25 years ago. I consequently recommend allocating investments by country market capitalization. You are getting additional GDP exposure through conglomerates that serve the underrepresented large economies.

Some mutual funds designate themselves as *tax managed*. These are like other mutual funds but with an additional constraint—they attempt to limit an investor's tax burden through a variety of techniques, like limiting exposure to dividend-paying stocks, limiting turnover to avoid recognizing capital gains, and matching gains with losses to minimize reported or taxable income. These strategies are appropriate for taxable investment accounts. They aren't a concern for IRAs and 401(k) plans.

■ Rebalancing Your Portfolio to Maintain Appropriate Market Exposure

Because the world economy and markets are dynamic, an investor must occasionally rebalance the portfolio to ensure that it reflects changes in market values and mimics the global weighting. In theory, rebalancing could be implemented continuously, but there are practical limitations related to the transaction and tax costs of rebalancing. The recommended practical compromise is to rebalance annually, or sooner if target allocations deviate from the target by 5 percentage points or more. Based on historical return and volatility assumptions, this basic rule results in a manageable number of rebalancing events with minimal transaction costs and tax leakage.

Several aspects of the Family Inc. investment program minimize the need to rebalance more frequently. Most investors contribute to savings throughout the year. These savings can be used to rebalance the portfolio without the transaction or tax leakage costs by simply buying more of the investment whose desired percentage of the portfolio has shrunk. For a portfolio heavily invested in index-based products, much of the rebalancing among countries occurs automatically as the index tracks the underlying markets. Targeting fixed income as an absolute dollar amount instead of a percentage of the portfolio also reduces the frequency of needed rebalancing.

■ Key Conclusions

Combining a U.S. and an international ETF or index fund produces maximum diversification at rock-bottom fees.

Even domestic funds provide meaningful exposure to international economies since a large percentage of U.S. corporate sales and earnings come from abroad.

Diversification among world economies should generally track the market capitalization of these markets. Today, the United States, developed international, and emerging markets represent approximately 50, 38, and 12 percent of the global market, respectively.

Rebalance the portfolio periodically to restore the desired proportions of each investment. The most efficient way to do this is to invest new savings into the securities that have lost ground.

CHAPTER 15

Understand When It Makes Sense to Pick Individual Stocks and Managers

Despite the advantages of indexed investments, many investors like to play a more active role on their own or with the assistance of a financial adviser. This chapter covers three active investment management scenarios: (1) investment selections by the Family CFO, (2) actively managed broker accounts, and (3) actively managed mutual fund accounts. With minor exceptions, the general recommendation for all these scenarios is the same: Don't do it!

■ Active Management by the Family CFO

As a professional investor, I usually reserve 5 to 10 percent of my portfolio for my own investment ideas. These investments are often simply an extension of my observations from work, where I have significant time, resources, and a network of professionals to assist in evaluating these opportunities. For most Family CFOs, I do not recommend such an approach, for several reasons:

- Unique investment ideas are opportunistic by nature and are usually difficult to manage in the context of a disciplined asset-allocation strategy.

- As Table 15.1 shows, the investor community as a whole is pathetically poor at predicting stock market performance. There's a strong inverse correlation between investor optimism, or pessimism, and how stocks later move. Essentially, the market as a whole has a predisposition to buy high and sell low—not a strategy for success.

- Even investors who are skilled at identifying attractive buying opportunities do not always stay current with all the relevant market and company information over time, and as a result aren't as good at selling as at buying. Selling an overvalued asset can contribute to a positive return just as effectively as buying an undervalued one.

- Trading success (buying and selling securities efficiently) is a product of judgment, information, and the speed with which the information can be processed to develop conclusions and take action. Even individual investors who possess the required judgment are bound to be disadvantaged on the information and speed fronts.

TABLE 15.1	The Confidence Trap—Investor Confidence and Subsequent Dow Jones Average Performance
	1970–2006
SENTIMENT (Higher=More Optimistic)	DOW JONES CHANGE 12 MONTHS LATER
0.2–0.3	20.47%
0.3–0.4	15.82%
0.4–0.5	13.43%
0.5–0.6	10.21%
0.6–0.7	6.03%
0.7–0.8	6.74%
0.8–0.9	−1.79%
0.9–1.0	−10.18%

Source: jeremysiegel.com.

- There is no accountability in this type of investing, with no clear benchmarks to rate your performance. What is the appropriate performance metric? How much risk did you assume to achieve your return? What peer group should be used for comparison purposes? In other words, it's hard to know if you are really any good at stock picking.

- Individuals often don't have the conviction to follow through with an investment thesis and are unduly biased by short-term fluctuations. In other words, investors—including me—often allow emotion and sentiment to unduly influence their decisions.

We often make mistakes that are a product of our personalities. I find that the biggest challenge for most investors is not the fear of loss, but rather the fear of being different. This has never been my challenge. As an impatient contrarian, my biggest mistakes have come from my inability to do nothing. One sad example (there are way too many to list them all!) occurred in the late 1990s. The environmental services (trash hauling) industry was consolidating, and Waste Management, Inc., was one of the darlings of this trend. For many reasons, this was a compelling investment and growth story. The demand for these services is consistent and growing. Waste Management could grow quickly through accretive acquisitions as it purchased the small mom and pop businesses in its territories. The stock seemed an attractive way to place a bet on the expanding economy of the late nineties.

In the summer of 1999, however, Waste Management announced a multibillion-dollar write-down of earnings related to improper accounting treatment of acquisitions. Within months, the stock lost approximately 70 percent of its value. This impairment resulted in a real credibility issue for management, clouding the company's prospects. I believed, however, that the market was overreacting. There was still a good, defensible business here in an industry that was growing and would continue to consolidate. I concluded that the long-term prospects remained bright while the near term was likely to be challenging, so I bought the stock in the fall of 1999 when the rest of the world was entranced by the great Internet boom. My assessment in 1999 was absolutely correct: Waste Management was a good business in a growing, rapidly consolidating market with attractive long-term prospects. Those investors who were able to look past the near-term volatility were rewarded handsomely: By 2006, the stock had appreciated by 275 percent.

Unfortunately, I never realized this gain because I didn't have the staying power. For the first year after my investment, the stock was a mess. More negative earnings announcements, shareholder litigation, and management turmoil all created a challenging environment. I sold out about a year after my investment and was happy to get *most* of my money back (that's a nice way to say this was a loser). The noise of the market was just too much for me to resist—negative research reports, negative news stories, and watching my investment sitting in the red all caused me to abandon my thesis too soon.

■ Actively Managed Broker Accounts

As with do-it-yourself stock picking, I generally oppose broker-managed accounts. The primary role of investment advisers (how they get paid) is asset collection, not security selection. The skill set of a good financial adviser—sales—is not necessarily consistent with being a good investor. Advisers who are paid on the basis of transaction and management fees have an inherent conflict of interests. Financial advisers who actively manage accounts often unnecessarily drive trading activity, generating fees and tax leakage. As with self-chosen securities, there's no real accountability associated with this approach, either. It's difficult to benchmark your financial adviser's performance versus the appropriate peer group.

■ Actively Managed Funds

I argue in the previous chapter that actively managed funds for inefficient and emerging markets can make good economic sense. *Nevertheless, I generally recommend that most investors avoid all actively managed funds in favor of low-cost alternatives.* While these recommendations may seem to conflict, they don't. My recommendation to avoid all actively managed funds is not based on a belief in efficient markets theory, which hypothesizes that markets fully price all information at all times so managers can never consistently outperform the markets. I have seen too many contrary examples in all types of markets and environments. I do believe that exceptional managers can consistently justify their expense regardless of market through increased return with less risk. However, I also believe that most individuals, probably including you as your Family CFO or your investment adviser, lack the skills and resources to differentiate between good fund managers and bad fund managers.

In practice, investors often chase returns by picking a fund manager with eye-catching recent performance without determining whether the return came from asset-class performance—the stock market rose or fell, for instance—or superior management. This habit often results in buying into an asset class right at the top of the market.

Picking a good manager is equivalent to identifying alpha (finding a manager who delivers a better-than-average return without taking incremental risk). By definition, this selection process is a zero sum game—for every manager who exceeds the asset benchmark, there is one who underperforms. As a professional in the business, I often find evaluating investment managers harder than evaluating investments directly because the criteria are much more nuanced. Furthermore, retail customers generally get little to no access to the fund manager or the strategy other than what's in the marketing material. Historical returns are not a compelling indicator of future returns. One study of data over 20 years showed that fewer than 50 percent of actively managed mutual funds that ranked in the top quartile in a three-year period went on to rank even in the top half in the next three-year period. This makes manager selection for the retail investor particularly challenging.

If you nevertheless choose to select an active fund manager, I recommend the following criteria in order of importance: continuity of the management team; a clear, consistent strategy over the years; a significant personal financial commitment to the fund by the team; a long-term investment philosophy emphasizing low turnover and low tax leakage; good benchmarking comparisons against the peer group; and moderate size of assets under management. The definition of moderate size depends on the market on which the fund focuses but is generally between $500 million and $5 billion. The larger a fund gets, the more likely it is to mimic the broader market, resembling an index fund but with higher fees.

If you determine that you want to invest in individual securities on your own or through a broker, I recommend no concentration in any single security in excess of 5 percent. That's 5 percent of your investable financial portfolio, not 5 percent of your Family Inc. Net Worth.

▆ The Unfortunate Reality of the Investment Management Game

Groucho Marx once joked, "I don't want to belong to any club that would have me as a member." Unfortunately, most of America might want to take the same view when selecting investment advisers. Because advisers are paid on the basis of how much money they manage, the best and most experienced managers manage the very largest accounts. As a result, most of the "aspiring wealthy" are left working with advisers of mediocre talent or promising young advisers who are essentially learning on your dime. It's hard to get a competent adviser to actively focus on your financial needs until you have at least several million dollars of investable assets or at a minimum demonstrate high income potential. This is yet another important reason that you can't outsource your responsibilities as the Family CFO.

■ Recommended Role of Your Financial Adviser

In identifying the weaknesses and conflicts inherent in the financial adviser community, I do not suggest that all advisers are bad or that they cannot play an important role in your financial planning activities. I have found financial advisers helpful in the following areas:

- Assisting in developing an asset-allocation framework consistent with your circumstances.

- Identifying low-cost passive funds such as ETFs for efficient markets and, sometimes, higher-cost active funds for inefficient markets.

- Administering and managing tax-advantaged products such as IRAs, 401(k)s, and 529 plans.

- Advising on insurance needs and tax planning.

- Planning for significant expenditures such as house purchases, vehicles, and college education.

- Providing an objective, unemotional sounding board as you navigate your financial plan.

- Providing general information and education about the markets and financial planning.

Assuming your investment adviser can provide these services at reasonable costs, the relationship can add real value. But approach any adviser with a healthy dose of skepticism. Don't follow recommendations blindly. Make the adviser convince you of the logic and the fit of each recommendation with your overall circumstances and risk profile. Demand fee transparency so you can understand any potential conflicts or motivations associated with the advice you are getting.

As you develop your financial needs, it's quite possible that you will need a team of specialists, including a financial adviser, a lawyer for estate planning, and an accountant for tax planning. While this requires managing several relationships, the unique expertise each adviser brings can make it worthwhile.

Some people also farm their financial portfolio out to multiple advisers. I recommend against this. We have seen over several chapters why financial advisers should not be used to make specific security selections. Use indexing or specific mutual fund managers for that. Your financial adviser can be of most value to you if he or she understands the entire financial picture when providing advice on major decisions such as asset allocation and retirement savings. This broad perspective on your financial goals, risk tolerance, and current circumstances is best accomplished through the use of one adviser.

■ Key Conclusions

Picking stocks yourself or having a broker or an active manager of a mutual fund do it for you usually produces investments that trail the market averages.

Even for inefficient markets such as emerging-country equities, most investors will do best by sticking to ETFs or index funds.

While generally not recommended as a selector of specific investments, a skilled financial adviser can usefully advise the Family CFO on an array of other financial decisions.

CHAPTER 16

The CFO's Step-by-Step Guide to Building the Family Investment Program

125

When we combine the Family Inc. paradigm with the principles of asset allocation and real-world investment results, we derive a financial management plan that is simple to understand and simple to implement, but dramatically different from the conventional consensus financial plan. Here are the 11 core tenets of the Family CFO investment program, in order of priority.

1. The first investment in the family business should be purchasing required life, disability, and umbrella insurance to protect your present labor and financial assets.

2. All capital assets (yes, 100 percent) should remain in cash and cash equivalents (savings accounts, short-term U.S. Treasuries, money

market funds, and the like) until you accumulate three to six months of living expenses. Include your cash plus available credit from a home equity line if you have one. This obligation should be funded even before you pay down debts. It is designed to provide the liquidity to satisfy the two most important functions of your asset management business—providing a safety net and financing working capital for Family Inc. I have specified a minimum of three months' consumption for the liquidity fund, but this can be customized on the basis of your job security. If that's uncertain, or if you have job requirements that might make finding a replacement job difficult, this cushion could be as much as 12 months of consumption. For most people who find themselves unemployed or injured, however, three months should be adequate given expected unemployment benefits or disability insurance payments.

3. Elect the maximum contributions to your employer-sponsored retirement program. Then elect to invest in U.S., international developed-country, and emerging-market index funds or ETFs in proportion to the relative market capitalizations of these markets (recently about 50, 38, and 12 percent, respectively). Tax deferral and employer matching programs make investments in retirement programs compelling. Retirement programs allow individuals to benefit from compounding pre-tax investments and deferring tax liabilities until the assets are consumed. As Table 16.1 shows, the combination of this deferral with employee matching programs, where available, and an investment portfolio biased toward equities will generally result in an increased expected after-tax annual return of 1 to 2 percentage points and a significant increase in the final value of assets over the No-401(k) alternative shown, depending on employee matching and tax assumptions.

4. Repay all debts other than those related to education, real estate, and long-term assets such as automobiles. Generally, loans outside those categories are relatively expensive, so paying them off as soon as possible is equivalent to making an investment that guarantees more than 5 percent after tax without the risks of the markets.

5. Invest all remaining capital in indexed equity. As discussed in Chapter 8, this significant exposure to stock markets makes sense given most families' structural overallocation to nonequities (labor assets, Social Security, and real estate), combined with the relative

	SCENARIO I	SCENARIO II	SCENARIO III
TABLE 16.1 401(k)s Make Investments Surge	No 401(k)	401(k)	401(k)
		No Employer Match	30% Employer Match
Employee's investment	$10,000	$10,000	$10,000
Employer match			$3,000
Taxes on investment	−$3,000	0	0
Total invested	**$7,000**	**$10,000**	**$13,000**
Value in 30 years*	$32,491	$46,416	$60,340
Tax liability at sale	−$5,098	−$11,604	−$15,085
After-tax value	**$27,393**	**$34,812**	**$45,255**
Multiple of capital	2.7	3.5	4.5
% Gain vs. no 401(k)	-	27%	65%
After-tax real IRR	3.42%	4.25%	5.16%

*Based on 5.5% pre-tax real return, fees of 25 basis points over 30 years, 25% income tax, and 20% capital gains tax.

attractiveness of equities for investors with long-term horizons. As with the 401(k), your indexed allocations should be diversified in accordance with the relative market capitalizations of world markets.

6. Investors who have access to, and can effectively evaluate, alternative equity strategies such as private equities and merger arbitrage strategies should target between 5 and 15 percent of their equity portfolios to these vehicles. Alternative strategies have greater expected returns, and their gains and losses show low correlations with public markets. But avoid these investments unless you're confident you can evaluate them and are quite sure that you won't need access to this capital in the short term. Private equity can offer superior returns, but it's by definition illiquid. To effectively manage this illiquidity, investors need adequate liquidity among other assets.

7. Including the 3 to 12 months of contingency cash established in item 2, I recommend a modified target for fixed income equal to three years' consumption minus the present value of remaining

labor (how far you are from anticipated retirement). So long as you are more than three years from retirement, there is no need for more fixed income exposure. Once you get within three years of anticipated retirement, the concept of the contingency reserve changes. You should start then to think about this reserve's serving two purposes—it's still contingency or emergency capital but it's also the source of funds you will soon use to live on. Near and after retirement, you should continue to add fixed income so that you always maintain three years of consumption capacity through a combination of anticipated labor income and fixed income investments.

From the time you retire, I recommend maintaining the 36-month reserve in the form of Treasuries, money markets, and municipal, corporate, and government bonds. To calculate the amount needed, start with your assumed consumption over the next three years and deduct the after-tax proceeds from guaranteed payments such as a pension, annuities, and Social Security. This recommendation, which for most retirees is for less fixed income than conventional rules of thumb propose, frees up incremental capital from fixed income to deploy to higher-returning equities while providing liquidity to ride out most stock market downturns without having to sell depressed equities. Based on history, if the money you'll need for the fourth year of consumption remains in equities for the next three years, it most likely will accumulate to approximately 115 percent of the current value in real terms, with a 68 percent likelihood that it will deliver between 85 and 150 percent of your initial investment in real terms. These are reasonable risk profiles for most investors. It is possible, of course, that this extra equity exposure could result in a loss during any three-year period. But during the course of your retirement you will be taking this chance many times, making the cumulative probability of loss acceptably low over your entire investment horizon.

8. This investment program recommends no publicly traded equities that are actively managed by mutual funds, brokers, or personal discretionary accounts. While actively managed public equity strategies sometimes outperform indexes, most individuals are poorly qualified to identify or administer superior

active management programs. To the extent the Family CFO is unusually positioned to identify outlier managers or investment opportunities, actively managed public equities can be an attractive addition to the portfolio. But if you embrace this type of program, do so recognizing that the long-term odds are against you.

9. To the extent possible, keep any actively managed equity products and alternative equity, as well as fixed income investments, in your tax-deferred accounts such as IRAs and 401(k)s. This will minimize the tax leakage associated with these products.

10. Use annual contributions to savings as a way to rebalance equity and fixed income targets.

11. Plan for significant purchases or capital reallocations. The preceding rules are helpful, but they don't acknowledge that throughout a family's life cycle certain decisions or events will cause dramatic reallocations of assets. Examples are managing inheritances and planning for large purchases such as a home or education. A family that assumes it will start tapping its investments in retirement, and so has only its contingency fund in cash or fixed income securities, may decide it soon wants to buy a house. Plans need to change to move much of the anticipated down payment into cash to fund the large near-term expenditure. At this point, minimizing the volatility of the money required outweighs the return opportunity.

For these events, I recommend multiyear planning similar to the framework provided in point 7. For example, if you find yourself overallocated to fixed income by 30 percent because of an inheritance, I recommend a 10 percent annual reallocation over three years to get to your target. While this pace may cause you to lose some potential gain, it insulates you from stock market crashes and bubbles while reallocating. For significant purchases such as a house, I recommend a similar strategy: Move your anticipated down payment to fixed income over the three years preceding your planned purchase. (Remember that at no time does a house purchase make the list of investment priorities. A family might be right to buy a house, but we must acknowledge that it is more a consumption decision than an investment decision.)

■ Reality Check

How can these 11 recommendations be sound when they are so different from the conventional wisdom? They are indeed far from the consensus view among financial advisers. The differences result from two significant factors:

1. Including labor and Social Security assets in the net worth and asset-allocation frameworks dramatically changes the outcome. While intellectually correct, this is not commonly done by advisers.

2. Perhaps more important, financial advisers and fund managers are generally paid on the basis of assets under management. The easiest way to increase the assets they manage is to avoid customer attrition or turnover. The surest way for an adviser to get fired is to lose a client's money, even temporarily, or fall behind the competition. Since this performance is measured annually, many financial advisers and money managers are myopically focused on outperforming the market on an annual basis even at the expense of long-term performance. Said differently, minimizing portfolio volatility is good business for the financial adviser even if it results in suboptimal asset allocation for the client. Sound investment advice for the individual may be bad business for the adviser.

User beware: This step-by-step guide will result in an equity-rich portfolio that is likely to produce better long-term outcomes with greater short-term volatility—so long as you stick with it. If you don't believe you have the discipline to stay invested when you encounter this volatility, simply increase your contingency reserve and fixed income retirement target and implement the rest of the program as recommended. With this additional reserve, you are likely to accumulate less wealth, but that's better than abandoning the program during volatile markets.

CHAPTER 17

Know Yourself—Understand the Psychological Factors That Can Torpedo Your Goals

Bill, a good friend of mine, is a senior manager at a well-regarded financial advisory firm. Given that many of my recommendations are unconventional, he and I have had many lively debates over the years about our disparate views on personal finance topics. Bill has also been a great source of feedback for me while writing this book. His biggest objection to many of my conclusions is not that my analysis and recommendations are wrong, but rather that the average person is incapable of executing my plan. In his view, most of us aren't disciplined enough to manage our finances as I recommend and, in particular, most of us don't have the intestinal fortitude to stay the course when the market and my investment approach deliver a shocking one- or two-year loss.

Bill's criticism of my plan is a legitimate concern. I believe, however, that through education and logic, people can be coached to the right actions. The preceding chapters have attempted to provide a logical framework for understanding the risks you face as the owner of Family Inc. The hope is that this framework nurtures the courage to stay the course during challenging investment environments. That courage can be strengthened by understanding certain psychological pitfalls or biases that can undermine rational decision making related to money. Consider the following 10 examples, each of which can be hazardous to your wealth.

Ownership bias. People tend to value things they already own more than those not yet owned. Example: We have friends who have had a house on the market for over a year and just can't figure out why it doesn't sell. The problem, however, is obvious to everyone else—it's overpriced. Lesson: Don't fall in love with assets. If you have decided to sell something, the best way to determine value is to listen to the market.

Sunk-costs bias. A sunk cost is a cost that has already been incurred and cannot be recovered. Example: I was once awarded a three-night stay at a resort that I had no interest in visiting. But I found myself worrying about passing up the value of those nights, and I was so reluctant to waste the money that I spent $1,000 to get there. Lesson: Sunk costs are just that. You can't change them, so don't let them influence your future actions. By staying home, I would have saved $1,000 and avoided three unmemorable days.

Budgeting bias. People often budget in a way that is biased toward missing their savings goals. Families are likely to miss their budgeted targets by overspending for some unanticipated expense rather than by underspending. Why? For most people, income (salary, bonus, and the like) is relatively predictable, but unanticipated expenses such as the car breaking down, a plumbing problem, a leaky roof, or an unanticipated sports camp for your kid are not easily foreseen. Lesson: If you want to achieve your savings goal, build in some contingency spending for unexpected expenses.

Lump sum bias. People are often better stewards of monthly paychecks than of large payments from commissions, bonuses, or equity gains. For some, these payments feel more like windfalls—found money—and recipients are likely to use this income to splurge on large-ticket items such as cars and vacations. Lesson: I recommend doing nothing with this income for at least six months. Only then, with the passage of time (and ensuring you have made any associated tax payments), decide how to spend or invest this asset.

Deal bias. Some people get satisfaction not so much from what they buy as from the act of getting a bargain. But as Thomas Jefferson wisely advised, "Never buy a thing you do not want because it is cheap." Lesson: Limit the impact that bargains have on your consumption. They often result in unnecessary spending.

Compartmentalization bias. Many of us create artificial constraints between the financial activities of our life. Example: We recently refinanced our house, which resulted in lower monthly payments. Because of this, Michele wanted to use this money to buy new furniture since our house budget was healthier than expected. But our total spending was overbudget. Lesson: Money is fungible. Creating "buckets" with money can distract you from your larger goals.

Size bias. Small numbers can have outsize consequences. As we saw in Chapter 9, annual management fees and expenses of 2 percent might look almost immaterial in relation to your total investment, but if we describe that difference as one-third of investors' historical inflation-adjusted gains, most of us would consider that material. Lesson: Don't be fooled by barely noticeable differences.

Hindsight bias. Once an outcome is in hand, people tend to believe the conclusion was obvious. Example: it's obvious today that Internet stocks were a bubble in 2000 and the markets were massively undervalued in 2009. At the time, these circumstances were not so obvious. Lesson: Don't be overconfident that the markets have reacted the way you thought they would. You may well have a biased recollection of history.

Loss aversion bias. People tend to feel the pain of loss more acutely than the joy of gain. Losing $100 at a casino creates stronger emotions than winning $100. Lesson: Loss aversion can cause you to be more conservative than you should be. When managing Family Inc., we aren't trying to optimize psychological well-being; we are trying to optimize financial well-being.

Extrapolation bias. People often wrongly take recent performance as the most likely indicator of future performance. Example: "Technology stocks are up big this year so I am buying in." Lesson: Every dog has its day. Asset classes generally demonstrate reversion to the mean, so extrapolating recent performance can be dangerous. Don't let current events and short-term information unduly affect long-term decision making.

My hope is that through awareness, you are more likely to avoid these biases in your own decision making. Thanks, Bill—we still disagree, but you have honed my thinking along the way!

CHAPTER 18

Don't Sweat the Details of Your Asset Management Business

When faced with the question of how to compete in the highly competitive game of asset management, the answer is: Don't. Your path to success is *not* playing the traditional game. The large investment houses of the world are well resourced with the best minds of researchers, analysts, and strategists. They have the most and best access to information and can act faster with big dollar movements than any individual.

Your only chance of success against this competition is to change the game. They are playing a game characterized by active management, high turnover, and overexposure to fixed income and U.S. equity markets, emphasizing one-year returns. If you follow the advice in this section, you will play a game of passive management with low costs and low turnover, more exposure to international markets, and minimal exposure to bonds and other fixed income—because you already have plenty of income exposure from your labor assets and Social Security benefits. Your risk-adjusted return will be optimized for a much longer period consistent with when you will actually consume the capital.

By pursuing this strategy, you may accept greater year-to-year fluctuations in portfolio value, but history shows in compelling fashion that over the long term, the compounding effect of the excess gains dwarfs the risks associated with this strategy. Table 18.1 summarizes the impact over an appropriately long period—a 65-year working and retirement lifetime— by comparing two scenarios. The traditional scenario is representative of a standard asset-allocation model (100 minus age for equity exposure) with active management, relatively frequent trading, and the associated expenses. The proposed scenario represents the recommended Family Inc. asset-allocation model for our sample family with a greater equity exposure and passive management limiting trading expenses and fees.

While Table 18.1 depends on assumptions that are subject to scrutiny, the conclusion remains firm. Traditional asset management models based on active

TABLE 18.1 How to Lose 70 Percent of Your Purchasing Power	Traditional	Proposed
Assumptions		
Nominal equity return	7.0%	7.0%
Nominal debt return	4.5%	4.5%
Inflation	1.5%	1.5%
Management fee	0.75%	0.20%
Annual portfolio turnover	100%	10%
Income tax rate	30%	30%
Capital gains tax rate	20%	20%
Duration (years)	65	65
Results		
Equity return after taxes, fees, and inflation	3.5%	5.2%
Debt return after taxes, fees, and inflation	1.1%	1.5%
Average debt allocation	58%	31%
Average equity allocation	43%	69%
IRR after taxes, fees, and inflation	2.17%	4.10%
Ending multiple of capital	4.0	13.6
Discount from Proposed Scenario	**−70%**	

trading (producing higher fees and taxes) and minimizing annual volatility through significant fixed income exposure result in dramatically less after-tax final value—approximately 70 percent less—than the Family Inc. Net Worth investment program based on significant equity exposure, low turnover, and low fees.

■ A Word of Caution—Time's Impact on the Quality of These Recommendations

As you evaluate the quality of the advice in this section, remember that the chances of success with this strategy increase with duration. This results from the simple trade-off of higher expected returns from equities at the expense of higher volatility. This basic insight results in an important caveat to the program: For this strategy to be consistently successful, it must be employed with an appropriate time horizon. In my view, that's a minimum of 20 years of anticipated equity ownership. Do you expect to be able to maintain this heavily equity-biased portfolio over the next 20 years without being forced to liquidate holdings other than for planned annual consumption amounting to less than 5 percent of the portfolio in any given year? Over this long a period an investor can have high confidence in capitalizing on the improved expected real returns with limited incremental volatility.

My parting comment regarding the management of your asset business harks back to my experience with Waste Management (Chapter 15). The biggest impediment to success is not deciding what to do, but rather having the conviction to do nothing. The plan recommended is simple and based on common sense and long-term results—so develop your version of it and stick to it regardless of what surprises the market provides.

Throughout this book, I preach the benefits of being able to adjust your financial plan over time to accommodate new information. Investments are one area in which you should be very hesitant to change your course. Decisions such as your savings rate, spending, and retirement age are all subject to change, but the core tenets of your asset allocation and investment strategy should stay firm. Adjusting your portfolio away from equities after a market correction is exactly the wrong maneuver. Adjust your operating assumptions as needed, but stay the course with your investment plan in the knowledge that you are a long-term investor and history is on your side.

FAMILY INC.
DOES NOT
MANAGE ITSELF

Sections I through III focus on refining the primary business activities of Family Inc. and the actions required to maximize the value of each business. Section IV provides a variety of practical business techniques, tools, and analytic frameworks to assist you in effectively managing Family Inc.

CHAPTER 19

Create Tools and a Reporting Dashboard for Managing Family Inc.

141

The first step toward effectively analyzing and managing Family Inc. is to develop monthly, quarterly, and annual financial statements. Compiling these statements monthly is a helpful process. Like someone on a diet, the more regularly you measure your progress, the more likely you are to stick to your plan. The basic Family Inc. financial statements, which can be customized and modified over time to fit the individual needs of your business, must include a balance sheet and a cash income statement. Just as a securities analyst evaluates a corporation's health by analyzing the ratios in its financial statements, a Family CFO can develop valuable insights into the quality and management of Family Inc. These statements should be shared every year with numerous constituents—potential heirs, financial advisers, the trustee of an estate, or others to ensure they are up to date in case the Family CFO becomes incapacitated.

This chapter includes some examples of these statements and associated metrics, beginning with a family's monthly income statement. Your income and expenses will differ, of course, but these examples provide templates that are a starting point for monitoring your own situation. To personalize these templates to fit you and your family, see familyinc.com. A word of reassurance to nonfinancial readers: Because this chapter provides working tools, it necessarily gets into a finer level of practical detail as we move from principles and rules to basic techniques—in nautical terms, we're moving from the bridge to the engine room. You may choose to skip some of the details for now and come back to them when you need them. You have my permission.

■ The Family Inc. Income Statement

A monthly cash income statement (Table 19.1) tracks how you allocate your money across major categories in your budget. While many families prepare a budget, few actually follow through with periodic analysis of variances from the budget. Personally, I find actual income statements more interesting and predictive than budgets.

Note that this income statement categorizes expenses into three basic groups—(1) fixed (long-term commitments such as loans), (2) semi-fixed (expenses that can be reduced over time, such as insurance), and (3) variable (expenses that can be changed monthly)—because the nature of these budgeted expenses has implications for how you manage your business. Grouping expenses in this fashion allows you to do *margin analysis*—examining various categories' percentages of the family's total revenue, as listed in the graphic under "Budget Analytics." While every family's circumstances are unique, these analytics reflect principles to consider when evaluating your income statement.

Income (or revenue) concentration is the mix among sources of income—how evenly split are two spouses' incomes, for example. Generally, the closer this number is to 50 percent, the better. A low number indicates more stability, as revenue is derived from two professionals with different and independent earning profiles.

Surplus (savings) margin. Surplus and savings are two terms for the same thing. Surplus margin is the amount of cash surplus divided by revenue. It measures how much of a family's revenue contributes to net worth or, said differently, how much goes to savings after satisfying all expenses. This is the most important metric on the page. First, it is a measure of how efficiently you are able to turn labor assets into capital. The faster you save, the faster you expand the investments in your asset management business. Second, this margin is a measure of how much buffer against contingencies is inherent

TABLE 19.1 Sample Monthly Cash Income Statement

Revenue		Percentage of After-Tax Income
Spouse 1	$7,000	
Spouse 2	$5,000	
Tax estimate	35%	
After-tax income	**$7,800**	100%
Fixed Expenses		
Mortgage	$1,800	
Property taxes	$300	
Car payment	$350	
Credit card payment	$400	
Student loans	0	
Subtotal	$2,850	37%
Semi-Fixed Expenses		
Insurance (life, car, disability, etc.)	$350	
Phone/cable	$150	
Gas	$300	
Utilities	$300	
Country club dues	$200	
Miscellaneous house maintenance	$150	
Groceries	$1,000	
Subtotal	$2,450	31%
Variable Expenses		
Entertainment	$300	
Vacation	$300	
Clothing	$500	
Eating out	$500	
Kids' activities	$300	
Subtotal	$1,900	24%
TOTAL EXPENSES	**$7,200**	
Budgeted Cash Surplus/(Deficit)	**$600**	8%
Budget Analytics (see text)		
Income concentration	58%	
Surplus (savings) margin	8%	
Fixed cost margin	37%	
Semi-fixed cost margin	31%	
Variable cost margin	24%	
Fixed and semi-fixed charge coverage	1.47	

in your Family Inc. For example, a family with a 25 percent surplus margin could experience a 25 percent decrease of income and still maintain its consumption, while a family with a 10 percent surplus would either have to cut into savings or reduce spending by 15 percent.

Fixed expenses, semi-fixed expenses, and variable cost margins. From a business perspective, variable costs or expenses are preferable to semi-fixed costs, which are preferable to fixed costs. Variable costs give the business owner more flexibility to adjust spending if income falls. For example, if 80 percent of your costs are fixed, it would be impossible over the short term to reduce your consumption enough to accommodate a 25 percent decrease in income, while a family with mostly variable cost obligations could adjust quickly.

Fixed plus semi-fixed charge coverage ratio. This is simply a mathematical comparison of after-tax income to the sum of fixed and semi-fixed expenses. The higher the ratio, the better for financial security. In the sample report, the fixed plus semi-fixed charge coverage ratio of about 1.5 shows that current income exceeds fixed and semi-fixed costs by 50 percent. While every family scenario is different, I believe a fixed and semi-fixed charge ratio of less than 1.25 generally exposes the family to excessive risk of financial distress.

■ Adding a Balance Sheet

Income statement analysis should not be conducted without also considering a family's balance sheet, like the sample in Table 19.2. It can result in different conclusions. For example, a family with substantial liquid assets might prudently manage the income statement with a low fixed and semi-fixed charge coverage ratio because they could easily sell assets to offset any reductions in revenue.

A family balance sheet is simply a list of all of the family's assets and liabilities. The left side lists all the assets. These are grouped into major categories based on liquidity (ease of turning into cash). The categories include liquid securities, illiquid assets, restricted accounts, real estate, depreciating assets, estimated labor, and Social Security assets. The right side of the balance sheet lists all of the family's debts, specifying important attributes such as duration (long or short term) and interest rates. As the name implies, the right and left sides of the balance sheet must be equal, or balance. The difference between the family's cumulative assets and its debts is the Family Inc. equity value, or net worth.

TABLE 19.2 — Sample Family Balance Sheet

Date of Record
(to be updated monthly)

Assets		Liabilities		Max	Rate	Type
Liquid Accounts		**Short-Term Borrowings**		*Max*	*Rate*	*Type*
Banking/checking	$4,000	Credit Card 1	$20,000	25,000	9.0%	Floating
Cash equivalents	30,000	Credit Card 2	10,000	15,000	12.0%	Floating
Short-term fixed interest	20,000	Car Loans	45,000	NA	6.0%	Fixed
Subtotal	$54,000	*Subtotal*	$75,000			
Liquid Investments						
Investment accounts	$200,000					
Subtotal	$200,000					
Illiquid Investments						
Private investments	$25,000	**Long-Term Borrowings**				
Loans to family	10,000	Mortgage	$200,000	NA	4.8%	Fixed
Stock options	100,000	Home Equity Loan	25,000	$100,000	5.5%	Floating
Subtotal	$135,000	School Loans	$0	NA	6.0%	
		Subtotal	$225,000			
Restricted Accounts						
401(k) accounts	$250,000	**TOTAL LIABILITIES**	$300,000			
IRAs	100,000					
Subtotal	$350,000					
Real Estate						
Primary residence	$250,000					
Subtotal	$250,000					
Depreciating assets **(fair market value)**						
Illiquid home assets	$20,000	**FAMILY INC.**				
(furniture, etc.)		**NET WORTH**	$1,549,000			
Vehicles	40,000					
Subtotal	$60,000					
Labor						
After-tax present value	$400,000					
Subtotal	$400,000					
Social Security						
After-tax present value	$400,000					
Subtotal	$400,000					
		TOTAL LIABILITIES				
TOTAL ASSETS	$1,849,000	**AND NET WORTH**	$1,849,000			

TABLE 19.2 *Continued*

Balance Sheet Analytics

Measures of Wealth

Family Inc. Net Worth	$1,549,000
Financial Net Worth	$749,000
Financial Earning Net Worth	$689,000
Investment Assets	$989,000

Liquidity Analysis

Contingency capital	$54,000
Months' contingency capital	7.5
Borrowing capacity	$85,000
Months' borrowing capacity	11.8
Net debt	$246,000
Net debt to after-tax earnings	2.6
Net debt to investment assets	25%

Asset Composition			Liability Composition	
Labor	$400,000	22%	Short-term debt/total debt	10%
Social Security	400,000	22%	Long-term debt/total debt	90%
Investment assets	739,000	40%	Tax-deductible debt/total debt	75%
Residence	250,000	14%	Fixed rate loans to total loans	82%
Depreciating assets	60,000	3%	Weighted after-tax borrowings cost	3.17%
Total	$1,849,000	100%		

Measures of Wealth

Underneath the sample balance sheet is a group of key measures of wealth as well as a variety of tools and ratios to evaluate the balance sheet. Let's look briefly at each of these items.

Family Inc. Net Worth equals total assets minus total liabilities. This is the broadest definition employed for net worth. In addition to financial assets, it should include values for the family's expected after-tax future labor and Social Security assets.

Financial net worth equals total *financial* assets minus total liabilities. This more traditional definition of net worth amounts to Family Inc. Net Worth excluding labor and Social Security assets.

Financial earning net worth is financial net worth excluding all assets or durable purchases that lose value, or depreciate, with normal age and use.

The excluded assets include cars, trucks, motorcycles, appliances, electronics, and furniture.

Investment assets are the sum of all financial assets other than depreciating assets. This metric identifies the productive assets your business has working for you at any time.

In addition to tracking the growth of your asset management business through these measures of wealth, you should also manage the composition of the assets, liabilities, and liquidity on your balance sheet.

Liquidity Analysis

Liquid accounts include checking, cash equivalents, and short-term fixed income. These accounts provide liquidity to manage the daily cash needs of Family Inc. and to provide a safe store of value. They generate little if any gain on an after-tax basis, but are always immediately available as contingency funds should you have a significant unexpected shortfall in your income.

Months' contingency capital is the amount of your liquid accounts divided by your monthly expenses. If you became unemployed tomorrow with no income, this ratio expresses the number of months your liquid assets could support your current rate of consumption. In this case, the family has approximately 7.5 months of contingency runway. I generally recommend managing these liquid accounts and consumption to ensure a minimum of three months' contingency capital.

Borrowing capacity represents the maximum you could borrow from various sources of credit (mainly a home equity line and credit cards) after subtracting any outstanding balances. Like contingency capital, these loans can be a valuable source of liquidity when needed unexpectedly. I believe that undrawn home equity lines can legitimately be counted as contingency capital, and I would be comfortable reducing the contingency reserve dollar for dollar. A home equity line of credit is a long-term financial commitment that can't be pulled unilaterally by the bank, and it can be borrowed against and put into the bank as a cash account. I do not feel the same way about credit cards, which can be pulled unilaterally and aren't secured by any asset. They should be viewed as an additional source of emergency capital, not a replacement for contingency capital.

Months' borrowing capacity expresses the amount of your borrowing capacity divided by your monthly expenses.

Net debt equals total debt minus liquid accounts. It's a more refined measure of leverage because it acknowledges that the cash is immediately available to retire debt if needed.

Liquidity ratios. The balance sheet template also provides two basic liquidity metrics that should be evaluated together. *Net debt to after-tax earnings* represents the after-tax cash available to service debt before any consumption, while *net debt to investment assets* highlights the relationship between investment assets and debt. The net debt to after-tax earnings ratio is particularly sensitive to life cycles: A young family may have incurred significant debt to finance a residence and education but has yet to enter peak earning years.

Lower ratios represent more liquidity and a more conservative balance sheet. I generally recommend maintaining a net debt to after-tax earnings ratio below 6.0 (debt no more than six times annual after-tax earnings). This metric should decrease with age. Net debt to investment assets should be below 1.0. There are several situations in which these ratios don't hold, however, or in which you might satisfy only one or two of these guidelines. If consumption-related debt—whether for depreciating assets or for spending more than you earn—represents a significant portion of total debt, then your leverage ratios should be lower. In cases in which a family has purchased substantial real estate assets through debt financing, the cash flow metric (net debt to after-tax earnings) will likely miss its target because real estate may not generate any cash flow. But it does represent enduring value. In this case, you are fine as long as net debt to investment assets is appropriately low and your fixed and semi-fixed charge coverage ratio is appropriately high to endure unexpected expenses.

■ Asset Composition

Asset composition metrics compare investment assets with assets that are less liquid or productive, such as labor, a primary residence, and depreciating assets. Because the allocation between financial and labor assets is mainly a product of a family's age, it is often not very manageable, with one crucial exception. This analysis forces you to acknowledge that with each year that passes you have depleted another year of productive labor, so at a minimum you'd better have accumulated additional financial wealth to offset the depletion of your labor asset. The other balance sheet composition metrics reflect how well your financial assets fit the goal of maximizing productive investment assets relative to all other asset categories.

The central insight from these metrics is that your financial goal is not to save your way to retirement but rather to earn your way through investing in appreciating assets. Allocating resources to less productive assets dramatically reduces your expected return, which increases the savings needed to achieve financial security. As explained in Section III, assume that a diversified *equity portfolio* generates 5 percent real, after-tax, after-fee returns. A realistic expected return for *real estate* after taxes and all the other costs of ownership is 2.0 percent to 3.0 percent, assuming you give yourself full credit for the avoided cost of renting an equivalent property. A *vehicle* is probably the best example of a common depreciating asset. Assume a five-year ownership period; on average, cars and trucks lose approximately 60 percent of their original value. Expenses such as taxes, maintenance, inspections, and insurance may amount to an additional 3 percent of fair market value per year, so the total cost of ownership for a $40,000 vehicle over five years is $30,000. While the owner undeniably receives benefit through owning the vehicle, from a strict investment perspective, the numbers are pretty daunting: The $40,000 investment loses 75 percent of its value, implying a negative internal rate of return of 21 percent.

Having a high proportion of your investments in real estate and depreciating assets can create a meaningful drag on your return. Table 19.3 highlights the math.

TABLE 19.3   **Asset Composition (Lifetime Averages)**

Preferred Allocation		
	Allocation	Real Return
Investment assets	75%	5.0%
Residence	20%	3.0%
Depreciating assets	5%	−10.0%
Weighted average return		**3.9%**
Implied multiple of capital over 65 years		**11.65**

Suboptimal Allocation		
	Allocation	Real Return
Investment assets	50%	5.0%
Residence	35%	3.0%
Depreciating assets	15%	−10.0%
Weighted average return		**2.1%**
Implied multiple of capital over 65 years		**3.74**

In this example, the suboptimal allocation reduces expected growth by about 1.8 percentage points per year, which, when compounded over a long period (65 years in this scenario) cuts back the final accumulation of assets by almost 70 percent.

■ Liability Composition

The liability metrics are used to optimize the components of your debt according to the following principles: Maximize long-term borrowings over short-term borrowings; maximize tax-deductible borrowings over nondeductible borrowings; and minimize the after-tax cost of borrowings. In pursuing these objectives, the following are good rules of thumb with which to manage your liabilities.

Maximize real estate loans over all other debt. Mortgage loans generally provide the most appealing mix of long maturity, low cost, and tax deductibility.

Finance significant purchases such as automobiles and education with available loans so long as these rates are less than 6 percent (implies real cost of borrowing of 3 to 5 percent, given historical inflation rates). These types of debt are generally attractive because of government funding for education and because lenders for assets like autos have recourse to the asset (they can repossess the car if you don't pay). If you're going to buy a car, do so by exploiting cheap, relatively long-term capital provided by the manufacturer or a bank rather than deplete your valuable liquidity reserve.

When evaluating various financing options, compare fixed interest and variable rate loans. While variable rate loans usually start at a lower rate, they shift the risk of interest rate movements to the borrower. There are no absolute rules about the cost-benefit of this trade-off, but the more debt a family has relative to its investments and income, the less the family is able to absorb potential increases in interest costs. Cheaper variable interest rate debt is more appropriate for families with little debt relative to income.

Use your credit cards as a loan source of last resort. Because your credit cards are unsecured debt, they are usually the most expensive source of borrowings.

But do include your home equity line of credit as a potential source of cash to support your contingency planning program. This is best accomplished by getting the maximum available credit limit but minimizing borrowings.

Think hard before prepaying mortgages, education loans, and asset-based debt such as car loans. They are usually relatively inexpensive and offer significant liquidity by allowing you to invest the cash if you don't use it to pay down the loans. The added liquidity and flexibility are likely to prove valuable at some point in the life cycle of Family Inc.

Set Up a Financial Dashboard

Once you've established the Family Inc. income statement and balance sheet, you can also use the data to create and chart your progress toward your financial goals over time. Figures 19.1 through 19.5 comprise a graphic dashboard of the information on the sample financial statements.

An Owner's Manual

As you read this for the first time, it likely seems daunting and extensive. However, once you've created the reports, understood the analytics, and set up the graphics, this process takes less than 15 minutes a month to update and is critical in the journey toward financial independence. If you still find this process too arduous, reduce the frequency to quarterly, which will still provide much of the benefit with one-third of the work.

There are no correct or absolute answers. The appropriate budget and capital allocation decisions are a product of your family's circumstances. Modify the proposed metric levels by your risk tolerance and circumstances. For example, two tenured college professors can justify less contingency capital, lower fixed charge coverage ratios, and higher debt-to-earnings ratios than a commission-based salesman and a stay-at-home parent.

One of the most valuable benefits of the process is that it forces a family to critically review how it saves, spends, and finances major purchases. Knowing actual spending patterns allows a family to create a realistic budget. Avoid excruciating detail, as the information often doesn't result in additional insights, and adds tracking burdens.

In addition to monthly and annual budgeting, I recommend a family make a high-level five-year forecast. This forecast is not likely to be very accurate,

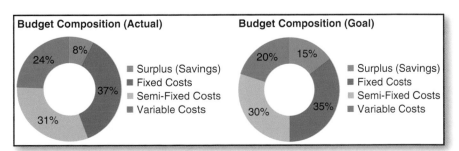

FIGURE 19.1 Income Statement Analysis

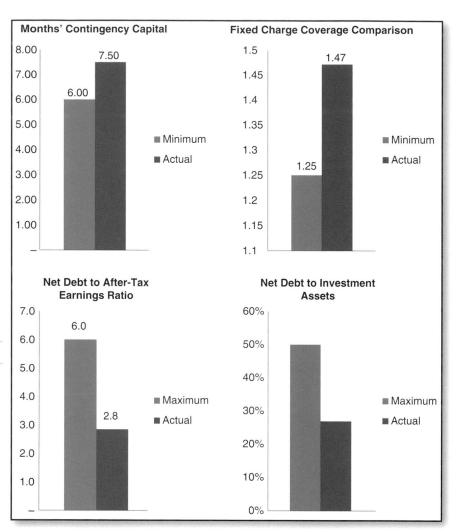

FIGURE 19.2 Liquidity Measurements

but the exercise forces the family to identify significant planned changes in employment and probable future investments, such as in education, vehicles, and real estate, and ensures that the short-term spending and saving plans are consistent with these significant investments. Some questions to consider include:

■ Do you anticipate any major career changes in the next five years—a different job or employer, significantly different compensation, a need for additional education or training?

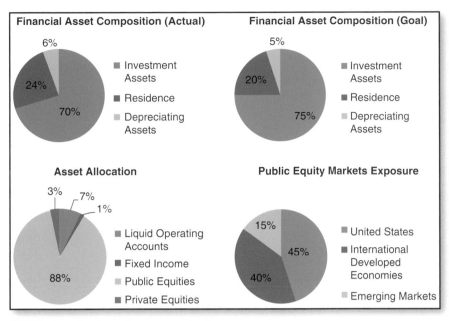

FIGURE 19.3 Asset Composition Analysis

- Do you plan any major purchases or financial commitments, such as a new house, a remodeling project, a car, a wedding?

- Do you expect any major windfalls in the next five years, such as an inheritance, sale of a business, or stock options?

- Do you expect any major changes in your expenses such as care for a new child or an elderly family member, or family educational costs?

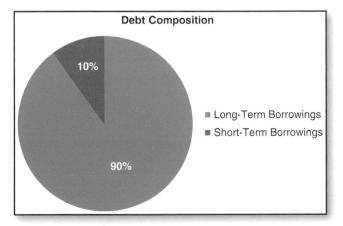

FIGURE 19.4 Liability Composition Analysis

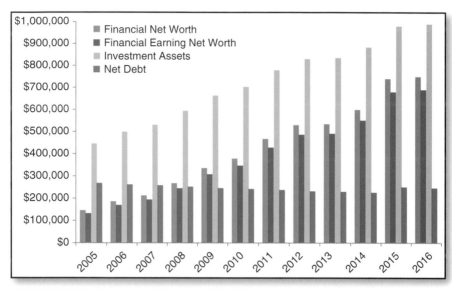

FIGURE 19.5 Tracking and Analyzing Net Worth

■ Employing Forecasting, What-If Scenario Analyses, and Monte Carlo Simulations

So far, all of the presented analysis has been historical, providing a vital snapshot of a family's current financial health. The real power of these tools, however, is that they provide the Family CFO with an accurate starting point and perspective to develop reasonable forecasts of what actions are required to meet financial goals.

Table 19.4 demonstrates how the Family CFO can conduct sensitivity analysis, also known as *what-if analysis*, about what actions are required to achieve a desired financial retirement goal and how changing assumptions or goals affects the likelihood of success. Major assumptions in this analysis include the retirement consumption goal, investment return, effective tax rate, Social Security benefit, and time until retirement.

We start with a person who wants to set a savings goal in order to be able to spend $65,000 in real terms annually (annual after-tax consumption) upon retirement in the next five to 10 years. This need is partially covered by assumed annual Social Security benefits of $24,000 pre-tax or $18,000 after tax, assuming a 25 percent effective tax bracket on the whole benefit. So the retiree will need to generate annual investment income of only $47,000 in addition to the after-tax Social Security income. Before being able to spend

| TABLE 19.4 | Two Routes to a Retirement Goal |

Desired After-Tax Consumption: $65,000 a Year

Option 1: Retire at 67

Assumed retirement date	12/31/2026	
Implied age	67	
Remaining years	10	
	Consuming Expected Return Only	**Consuming Principal and Return Thru 90**
Target principal at retirement	$1,253,333	$845,284
Current value of Earning Net Worth	$689,000	$689,000
Value of Earning Net Worth at retirement	$1,122,308	$1,122,308
Required incremental savings	$131,025	−$277,024
Required annual savings until retirement	$10,417	−$22,025
Present value of savings required to meet goal	**$80,438**	**−$170,069**

Option 2: Retire Five Years Earlier

Retirement date	12/31/2021	
Implied age	62	
Remaining years	5	
	Consuming Expected Return Only	**Consuming Principal and Return Thru 90**
Target principal at retirement	$1,253,333	$933,616
Current value of Earning Net Worth	$689,000	$689,000
Value of Earning Net Worth at retirement	$879,358	$879,358
Required incremental savings	$373,975	$54,258
Required annual savings until retirement	$67,680	$9,819
Present value of savings required to meet goal	**$293,019**	**$54,258**

Assumptions

Retirement goal: annual after-tax consumption	$65,000
Estimated after-tax Social Security benefits	−$18,000
Annual after-tax income required from savings	$47,000
Effective tax rate	25%
Required annual investment income	$62,667
Real return after fees	5%

$47,000, though, he or she will have to pay taxes on sold investments or withdrawals from an IRA or 401(k). So, assuming a 25 percent effective tax rate, this number must be grossed up to approximately $63,000 of required annual investment income (assuming most of the liquidated investments are in pre-tax 401(k)s and IRAs). In other words, withdrawing $63,000 from an IRA, along with the after-tax $18,000 from Social Security, would get the retiree to the goal of $65,000 of after-tax spending power for that year.

For ultimate security, many people would like to be able to live in retirement by spending only the expected annual returns on their investments without touching the principal. Table 19.4 shows that, in our example, the super-safe strategy would require saving hundreds of thousands of dollars more by the time of retirement. One alternative to this very conservative approach is to systematically spend down principal and returns over your expected retirement period (23 to 28 years from retirement age to 90 in these examples). This approach does raise a small but real possibility of outliving the money.

All those numbers reveal some important news: At 5 percent a year, the current value of financial earning net worth, $689,000, will compound to $1,122,308 by age 67. To achieve the stated retirement spending goal without spending principal, this investor must accumulate an additional $131,025 by 2026. This additional net worth could be achieved by saving $10,417 more per year through retirement or by investing a lump sum of $80,438 today.

Further sensitivity is provided by showing (Option 2) what savings would be required to achieve the same spending ability but with retirement five years earlier, at age 62. Annual savings must increase significantly from about $10,500 to more than $67,500. Both options also show the trade-off between assuming more risk of shortfall by spending down your assets and reducing the amount of required investment to support your retirement goal. Option 1 shows that if the plan is to retire at 67, the investor has already exceeded the required saving goal. Option 2 shows that spending down investments in retirement is probably the only realistic way to reach the retirement spending goal by age 62—and even so, the investor would need additional savings of almost $10,000 per year over the remaining five years.

As in Table 19.4 I often look at two scenarios when I think about how much capital is required to support some level of consumption.

1. Consuming only projected after-tax return. The left column indicates that approximately $1,250,000 at retirement will support almost $63,000 a year in liquidations (sales), assuming a 5 percent

real return, and meet the spending goal without depleting principal. This is the ultimate in financial security because you no longer have to make longevity assumptions. At your target spending levels and return assumptions, you cannot outlive your money.

2. Depleting your Financial Earning Net Worth over a projected retirement period. The right-hand column for Option 1 shows that a portfolio of $845,284 should support the same targeted liquidation amount of $63,000 a year from ages 67 to 90. In other words, a person who's willing to deplete principal in retirement needs about $400,000 less—and in this case can stop saving.

These calculations can be continually updated to reflect changes in your financial earning net worth, your anticipated future savings rates, and your duration of employment. In short, a sound understanding of your current financial earning net worth provides valuable visibility into your likelihood of achieving retirement goals as well as the trade-offs you may face.

As you determine which drivers of family net worth you want to exploit, it is helpful to understand how each affects the end result. The what-if analysis shown in Table 19.5 gauges the sensitivity of four major drivers of wealth accumulation on the basis of our initial family net worth scenario for a 25-year-old man: (1) salary, (2) savings, (3) investment return, and (4) retirement age.

This analysis is based on the assumption that the sensitivity changes affect the entire period. For example, savings increase from 10 to 12.5 percent from age 25 through retirement. The critical output from this analysis is the amount of implied annual withdrawals in retirement that can be funded by changing these inputs. Financial earning net worth, which will fund spending in retirement, is most sensitive to increases in investment returns and increases in retirement age. Increasing salary and increasing savings rates are often difficult and can come at the expense of quality of life—working harder and spending less. However, increasing investment returns with a sound low-cost, low-tax equity-heavy portfolio and choosing career options that allow you to work longer are relatively easy. As Table 19.5 shows, a one-point increase in investment return after inflation, taxes, and fees can result in an increase of approximately 39 percent in retirement spending. Extending your career by just three years (a 7 percent increase in your working life) increases projected retirement consumption by 30 percent. Most people's earnings are greatest during their last years of work, and extending your work life allows your investments to grow for an additional three years while also reducing future retirement spending by three years.

TABLE 19.5 **Which Changes Affect Retirement Income Most**

	Base Case	Increase Salary (by 10%)	Increase Savings (by 2.5%)	Increase Real After-Tax Return (by 1%)	Increase Retirement Age (by 3 years)
Assumptions					
Average lifetime salary	$68,723	**$75,595**	$68,723	$68,723	$71,094
Saving (after-tax salary)	10.0%	10.0%	**12.5%**	10.0%	10.0%
Real, after-tax return	5.0%	5.0%	5.0%	**6.0%**	5.0%
Retirement age	67	67	67	67	**70**
Results					
Net worth at retirement	$567,381	$624,119	$709,226	$721,106	$679,813
% change		*10%*	*25%*	*27%*	*20%*
Consumption through age 90	$42,064	$46,270	$52,580	$58,610	$54,550
% change		*10%*	*25%*	*39%*	*30%*

While this sensitivity analysis provides important insights, its static nature is a significant limitation. The analysis neatly assumes that real returns on your investments after taxes and fees are 5 percent per year and you live to be exactly 90. While these are reasonable assumptions supported by history, they are most likely wrong. For this reason, I recommend also incorporating these assumptions into a Monte Carlo simulation. That analysis not only provides the Family CFO with a sense of the expected outcome, but also the variability around this expected outcome and the implied risk of shortfall.

As the Family CFO, you need not only to manage the averages, but also to understand the possible range of outcomes to ensure you have adequately accounted for the risks you may encounter. The projection in Figure 22.1 in Chapter 22 highlights the two major risks retirees face: volatile investment returns and life expectancy. Here, we use a Monte Carlo simulation to describe statistically how returns and life expectancy can vary around their averages. Figure 19.6 shows the simulation results for the possible compound annual return on your investments, assuming an average of 5 percent with a standard deviation of 2 percent. (Terms are defined in the Glossary at the end of this book.) The average return resulting from this simulation is 5.09 percent (very close to our 5.0 percent expectation), but as Figure 19.6

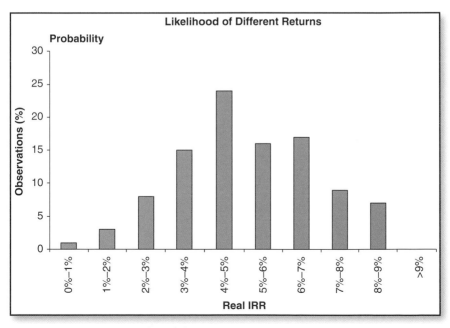

FIGURE 19.6 Monte Carlo Simulation

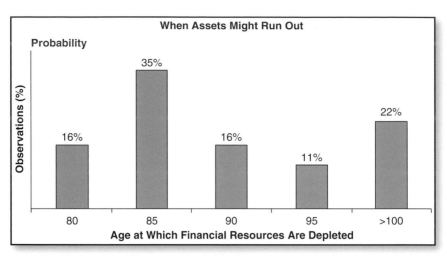

FIGURE 19.7 Monte Carlo Shortfall Simulation

shows, there are lots of examples in which returns were significantly better or worse; 51 out of 100 instances are below 5 percent.

Using these simulation results, we can estimate when our savings would be exhausted if we continue to liquidate our target of $63,000 per year (Figure 19.7). Not surprisingly, the expected time for the savings to be depleted is at age 90, but there is significant risk (51 percent of the time in the simulation) that the assets will be exhausted before the retiree turns 90.

Averages can also be deceiving when it comes to life expectancy. While the average life expectancies for a 67-year-old man and woman are 83 and 86, respectively, the ranges around these averages vary greatly. Figure 19.8

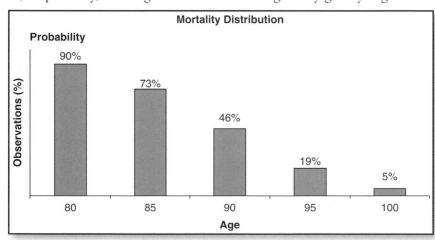

FIGURE 19.8 Probability That at Least One Member of a 67-Year-Old Couple Is Living at Various Ages

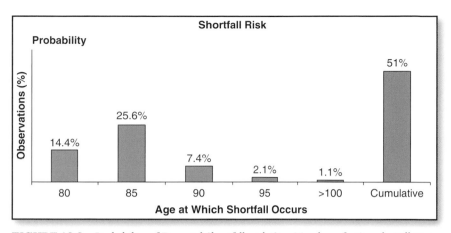

FIGURE 19.9   Probability of Financial Shortfall with One Member of a Couple Still Living

shows the probability that at least one member of a 67-year-old couple will be alive at various ages. The initial scenario assumed exhausting assets by age 90, which seemed conservative, but there is approximately a 46 percent chance that one member of the family will still be alive at age 90.

When we combine all that we know about expected returns and life expectancies as well as their variation around these expectations, this simulation shows (Figure 19.9) that there is a 51 percent chance that a 67-year-old couple who liquidate $63,000 per year from savings of $845,000 will exhaust their savings before both individuals die.

The goal of this simulation is not to scare you about the risks your financial plan faces, but rather to highlight that you cannot develop a plan simply based on the average expected outcome. You need a plan that will be successful or adequate for a reasonable range of outcomes, a plan that includes a cushion against the chance that your investment returns are low or your life unusually long. Using simulation, and continually updating your assumptions about how much you need to save or how much you expect to spend, is a powerful tool. We will address other ways to deal with this uncertainty in Chapter 21 with comprehensive retirement planning.

■ Understanding the Mathematics of Saving

When pursuing opportunities to cut spending, follow the money and focus on the big-ticket items.

Residence. As discussed in Chapter 8, a primary residence is usually one of the largest assets in the family portfolio and not a very good investment, with an expected annual return less than half the expected return for equities.

Given the magnitude of this investment and all the related consumption such as taxes, maintenance, utilities, and furniture, perhaps one of the best investments a family can make is *not* purchasing a bigger residence.

Children. Estimates for raising a child in the United States range as high as $250,000 from birth to age 18. This is not meant as advice to avoid parenthood, but rather as encouragement to consider cost as one of numerous factors in financial planning for this decision.

Vehicles. Cars and trucks represent a great example of how to save money, not by doing without, but simply by delaying a purchase. Depreciation is the largest expense in the early years of ownership, so buying a used vehicle or deferring the purchase of a new one can generate substantial savings.

The important theme is not reducing costs but rather making decisions that avoid costs. By avoiding large, long-term, nonessential capital investments, you can not only avoid substantial expenditures, you can also maintain the financial flexibility required to ensure security.

■ Beyond the Balance Sheet

Some intangible assets do not appear on the Family Inc. balance sheet and are often overlooked: reputation, relationships, education or professional certifications, your creditworthiness or credit score. Like any asset, these should be nurtured and developed in a way that maximizes your labor value and your access to capital.

From a financial perspective, two things in life are best done once—getting married and retiring. Deciding when to retire is often a deeply personal decision that encompasses many issues beyond the financial: job satisfaction, health, and the aspirations of your spouse among them. While I can't offer emotional and marital advice, I can offer the following observation: Financially, it's easy to retire too early but there is no such thing as retiring too late. This causes me to err on the side of caution. If I'm able, I would rather work a year or two longer to ensure that I have the financial cushion I need. Each year you defer retirement has a significant impact on your financial situation: You are generally near the peak of your earning potential, so every additional year near retirement often represents more than five times your initial annual income, and for every year you defer retirement, you have also reduced the years during which you must fund your consumption from your investments. It isn't easy going back to work once you have elected to retire; you may well encounter significantly less responsibility and less pay. If you have any doubt about the timing of your retirement, then you aren't ready!

▪ Key Conclusions

By refining your understanding of Family Inc., the tools in this chapter can help you make and stick to your plan. Income statements, balance sheets, and analytics are just as important to Family Inc. as they are to any business.

Be skeptical of averages when planning retirement. Averages are useful for determining the most likely outcome, but the deviations around these averages are often significant.

The decision regarding retirement timing is the single most important decision affecting how much you'll be able to spend in retirement. Typically, the last years of employment are some of the highest earning, so they often produce especially high savings, including increased contributions to retirement plans. And for every year you defer retirement, you have reduced your post-retirement financial needs by a year.

Because this decision is the one you can't afford to get wrong, err on the side of working too long. People often dream of retiring at some specific age. You should retire when you achieve the net worth goal required to support your retirement objectives.

163

MANAGE YOUR FAMILY ENDOWMENT IN RETIREMENT

Your family business changes in retirement, but there's still plenty to get right to optimize your assets, protect your spending power, and help your heirs. Section V provides the tools.

CHAPTER 20

Understand How Your Family Business Changes in Retirement

Upon retirement, the objectives and constraints of your asset management business change, and so must the way you manage your capital. During your career, as discussed in Chapter 7, the primary objectives of your asset management business include pursuing appreciation to support future consumption during retirement and providing contingency capital for unlikely and infrequent shortfall events. With a contingency reserve as a bulwark against forced selling of equities to cover a shortfall, investors can benefit by holding significant equity investments, accepting greater short-term volatility in exchange for greater long-term appreciation.

So long as you're actively employed, you can often mitigate financial setbacks by working longer or taking out a loan. Retirement is different. The objectives of the family asset management business and the family's risk tolerance change meaningfully. The primary objectives of your asset management business changes from providing appreciation and contingency capital to funding annual consumption while providing growth and appreciation for future years. This results in a shorter expected investment duration and less ability to withstand major volatility. At the same time, Family Inc. loses financial flexibility. You can no longer make up shortfalls by working more, and loans are harder to qualify for without an income. The nature of consumption also may change in retirement, with less emphasis on purchasing assets such as houses and vehicles and more spending related to necessities such as food and health care. The composition of your expenditures becomes more fixed in nature.

These changes demand a modified investment and consumption plan at retirement that appropriately balances competing demands.

- A spending rate that provides ample cushion to prevent running out of money before you die, but without unduly reducing your quality of life by saving too much.

- A portfolio that provides enough stability to fund annual consumption even in bad markets while also providing appreciation from significant equity exposure to fund future consumption.

The asset-allocation rules provided in Chapter 16 allow the Family CFO to effectively balance these competing demands. By basing the asset portfolio's fixed-income target on the family's consumption plans, the portfolio can provide near-term liquidity for consumption while preserving equity exposure for long-term gains in real purchasing power.

CHAPTER 21

Sleep Well— Protect Your Retirement through Insurance

169

In Chapter 6, we discussed how insurance could be used to hedge Family Inc. against the loss of labor potential—the family can buy life or disability insurance to compensate it should an adult die or become disabled before having an opportunity to turn the expected value of that labor into financial assets. Other types of insurance are relevant later in the life cycle of financial management. These include longevity insurance (annuities) and health-care related insurance products (long-term care and supplemental medical insurance).

■ Longevity Insurance

Longevity insurance pays out to offset the additional living expenses that are incurred when someone lives longer than anticipated. Figure 21.1 demonstrates that there's a good chance that one partner in a couple will live well beyond the statistical averages.

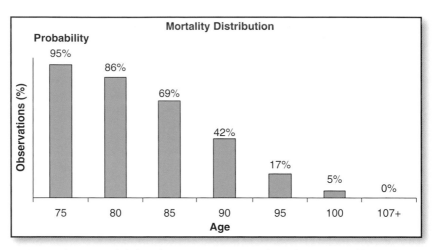

FIGURE 21.1 Probability That at Least One Member of a 50-Year-Old Couple Is Living at Various Ages
Source: Vanguard, 2011.

The uncertainty related to longevity, which can dramatically affect the quality of life for a retired couple, presents a significant planning challenge to the Family CFO. If you live longer than your financial plan assumed, you may exhaust your financial resources and have to rely on your children if you have them. On the other hand, if you take an extremely conservative approach and assume you or your spouse will live to be 100 (5 percent probability), this can cost the family dearly in forgone consumption.

Annuity overview. Longevity insurance is purchased through an annuity contract. In its most basic form, you make a lump sum payment today in exchange for a stream of future payments. Those payments can be a fixed amount for a specified time, such as 30 years, or until a specified event, such as the death of one or both spouses. Annuity payments can be indexed to a variety of metrics such as inflation or the performance of a portfolio of stocks. Appropriate indexes can ensure preservation of purchasing power for the recipient as well as potential gains when the equity markets outperform the guaranteed rate of return.

Because annuities are an insurance product, they have some unique tax attributes. Gains that occur before withdrawal are tax free, but distributions in excess of your principal are taxed as income. From an investment perspective, annuities are relatively fee inefficient, imposing asset management fees, insurance-broker commissions, and an embedded insurance premium. Some of this leakage can be eliminated by purchasing the product directly from the insurance company rather than through a broker.

Annuity economics. The payments from an annuity have three sources: return of part of your initial investment each year; interest on that capital; and "mortality credits." The credits benefit those who live longest. With a participating annuity, premiums paid by those who die earlier than expected contribute to gains for the overall pool of annuity holders. For holders who live longer, this mortality credit increases significantly with age and hedges longevity risk, often creating a return that would be impossible to match in the broader financial markets. This return is a perfect hedge for the increased expenses associated with living longer.

For purposes of evaluating annuity economics, we will keep it simple by using a traditional fixed income annuity for a 65-year-old male who makes a $100,000 investment today in exchange for annual payouts of $6,788 (6.8 percent of the initial investment). Figure 21.2 shows the components of this payout over time.

When an annuity holder dies determines the return on investment (IRR). The average 65-year-old male, such as the subject of Figure 21.2, is expected to live to about age 83. Over the 18 years from 65 to 83, the annuity payments would total $122,184, representing an internal rate of return of 2.2 percent. If the annuitant lives to be 100, the return improves to approximately 5.9 percent.*

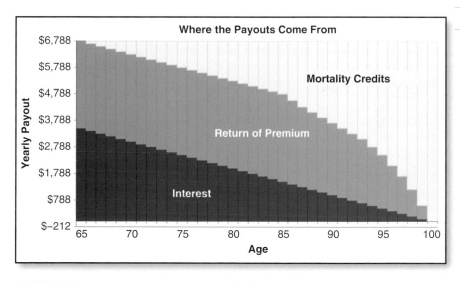

FIGURE 21.2 Components of Guaranteed Lifetime Annuity Payouts Male Age 65, $100,000 Investment

Source: Lawrence Petrone and Scott DeMonte, "Income Annuities Improve Portfolio Outcomes in Retirement," Financial Research Corporation, Boston, 2010. Data from New York Life based on rates as of April 1, 2010.

---

*The 6.8 percent cash payout includes return of principal, so IRRs are lower.

In isolation, I'm not enthusiastic about a 2.2 or a 5.9 percent annual return conditioned upon a 65-year-old living to 83 or 100. Yet in spite of this mediocre return, annuities—when purchased at the right price—possess attributes that can make them highly attractive within the family portfolio. Annuities provide a constant payment, which assists the retiree in planning and represents a perfect hedge against longevity risk—the longer you live, the more financial assets you consume and the more the total payout is delivered by the annuity. Fixed income annuities also possess zero correlation with the performance of other assets in your portfolio other than Social Security and, therefore, can provide valuable diversification. While this diversification is helpful, it's a distant second to the longevity hedge.

■ Techniques to Minimize Annuity Costs

Let's focus on two techniques to procure these benefits at a reasonable price.

Defer buying an annuity. When you buy an annuity relatively early in life, the likelihood that you will collect meaningful dollars is high, so most of your return goes to pay back your principal and interest. When you buy late in life, there is a good chance you won't collect as much on the principal and interest (your nominal rate of return on capital may drop)—but by definition you are getting more "insurance" (mortality credits).

The primary problem with the scenario in Figure 21.2 is that most of the return achieved by the investor is delivered through return of interest and premium. Investors can replicate the return of interest and principal with stocks and bonds without paying an annuity's high administrative costs. Buying a decade later, however, changes that. A 75-year-old male can procure the same $6,788 a year for the rest of his life for $76,270, a 24 percent price reduction. If he lives to age 85.5 (the life expectancy for a male at 75), the internal rate of return on this investment is −1.9 percent; if he lives to 100, that return increases to 7.4 percent. By delaying the date of his annuity purchase, he might get a lower expected return on his investment, but he can also increase the payout from mortality insurance, which more closely matches the costs associated with living longer.

Purchase an advanced life deferred annuity. This product is generally bought at retirement or earlier but doesn't begin to pay out until much later—age 85, for example. The long deferment period between purchase and payout is another way to leverage your premium dollar to procure a relatively cheap product. For the same $100,000 he paid for an immediate annuity, the 65-year-old in Figure 21.2 could purchase an advanced life deferred annuity with payout commencing at 85 that would generate an annual payout of approximately $62,000. By deferring the payment of the annuity benefit by 20 years, the purchaser increases the annual payment by more than nine times.

In fairness, both techniques are likely to deliver a similar expected return on investment, and both actually increase the volatility of the possible outcomes (how many payments you'll live to collect), something we attempt to avoid in the rest of our portfolio. But the difference here is that this volatility perfectly hedges the consumption needs of the family. If someone purchases the advanced life-deferred annuity at 65 and dies at 70, it will have been a horrible investment, but the money wasn't required anyway. If the buyer lives to be 100, it will have been an exceptional investment, generating an 8.5 percent IRR and 800 percent appreciation over the original investment. More important than the investment merits—let's acknowledge that the chances of anyone living to 100 are rather small—this investment perfectly hedges the increased consumption requirements resulting from an unexpectedly long life. Indeed, the guaranteed payout related to this product may allow you to take more risk with the rest of your portfolio by adopting higher withdrawal rates.

■ Rules for Annuity Purchase Programs

I recommend following rules when considering annuity purchase programs.

Self-insure if you're able. Given the fee and premium leakage, longevity insurance is most beneficial for families in which the possibility of outliving their assets is a real risk. To the extent that you have acquired enough wealth relative to your desired annual consumption that you are unlikely to run out of money regardless of how long you live, self-insurance works. (The next chapter includes more detail on how to determine if you should self-insure or annuitize.)

Buy annuities that maximize the ratio of longevity insurance to a guaranteed return. These are immediate annuities purchased relatively late in life (older than 65) or deferred annuities that don't begin paying out until much later. These provide the most leverage, defined as longevity insurance (mortality credits) per dollar of upfront payment.

Buy inflation-protected dual-longevity annuities. I recommend a product that provides a fixed annual benefit with an inflation adjuster to preserve real purchasing power and that continues payments so long as either spouse remains alive. Some annuities are structured to provide a reduced payment when one spouse dies, usually 50 to 75 percent of the initial benefit. Look for a reduction of no more than 25 percent; the cost of living does not go down proportionately when one spouse dies.

Rightsize your annuity. This insurance is designed to protect against hardship by providing the minimum income stream required should you deplete your other assets. I generally define the maximum annuity amount as your total monthly fixed costs minus your anticipated Social Security and any other defined payments, such as pensions.

Buy direct. To avoid high sales commissions, buy these products directly from the insurance company when possible.

Demand high credit quality. Because of the long duration of this product, buy an annuity only from the highest-rated insurance companies—no less than AAA from Standard & Poor's or A++ from A.M. Best. While companies with lower credit quality might offer a marginally better payout, this risk is unacceptable, given the need you are insuring.

Purchase annuities over time. You may want to purchase more than one annuity over the years. Interest rates, which determine payouts, change. So may your need for steady income and your view of your family's longevity. I strongly recommend diversifying these annuity purchases among several insurance companies for additional protection against the possibility that your carrier someday encounters financial distress and cannot meet its obligations to you.

Reduce the other fixed income exposure in your portfolio to account for increased annuity exposure. The guaranteed contractual nature of payments makes an annuity similar to a bond. So, for every dollar in annuities you purchase, you are increasing your fixed income exposure. While the annuity has many attributes of fixed income, it has a much longer maturity and does not serve as an effective asset for emergencies or contingencies. Even so, I would suggest decreasing up to one year of your three-year fixed income consumption target by the amount of annuities purchased. To preserve your ability to get cash regardless of the size of your annuity purchase, however, don't go below a two-year fixed income reserve excluding the annuity.

■ Rebuttal to Annuity Critics

Annuities have been surprisingly unpopular among most retirees despite the attractive attributes of longevity insurance. Here are some common concerns regarding annuities and my reactions.

I am concerned that if I die early, I won't get my money's worth. This is absolutely true, but if you die early, you won't need it.

Annuities are a bad investment; I can achieve a higher return by investing on my own. This may also be true, but there's great value in having longevity insurance that matches the incremental costs of living longer than expected. In addition to the expected return on the investment, it can be a reassuring hedge for the family.

Buying an annuity reduces my heirs' inheritance. This is flawed thinking. The present value of their expected inheritance is similar regardless of your insurance purchase, but the volatility of the expected inheritance is likely reduced by longevity insurance. For example, if you die early, your heirs would have received a greater inheritance had you not annuitized. However, the opposite is also true—if you live longer than expected, your heirs will inherit more than they otherwise would have. Moreover, if you avoid longevity insurance and deplete your assets, you may instead become a burden on your heirs, which I view as the worst possible scenario.

■ Social Security as an Annuity

In Section I, we noted that Social Security is essentially a government-mandated annuity. Indeed, it offers many ancillary benefits that are analogous to insurance riders (extra policy features), such as a lower tax rate on Social Security income (ranging from zero to 85 percent of your current tax rate, depending on total income), 100 percent survivor benefits for a surviving spouse who is of full retirement age, inflation adjustment of benefits, and additional benefits to support disabled family members who were supported by the deceased family member (up to 180 percent of the deceased's benefits). While you can't control how much you pay into Social Security, you can choose to start receiving benefits anytime between ages 62 and 70. Figure 21.3 shows how changing the starting date affects the monthly benefit for a recipient who is eligible for a $1,000 per month benefit at full retirement age (66).

By deferring your Social Security benefits from 62 to 70, you are essentially opting for a deferred annuity over an immediate annuity. As we have seen, that results in higher levels of mortality credits. You can't control the purchase decision for this benefit, but you can maximize its value by opting for the benefit offering the greatest mortality insurance.

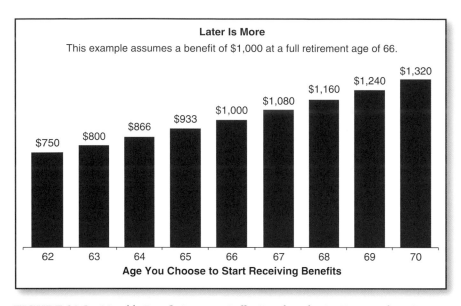

FIGURE 21.3 Monthly Benefit Amounts Differ Based on the Age You Decide to Start Receiving Benefits

Source: Social Security Administration, Publication No. 05–10147, January 2014.

▪ Health-Related Insurance Products

For a retired couple, average uninsured health-care costs, including Medicare Parts A, B, and D premiums and co-payments, averaged $8,600 a year in 2012. The present value of a 65-year-old couple's lifetime uninsured health-care costs, including nursing home charges, averaged $260,000 in 2009. (In other words, it would take an investment of $260,000 now to cover those expected lifetime costs.) There is significant variance around the mean lifetime health-care cost, however. The 95th percentile is projected to experience total lifetime costs of $570,000 in today's dollars. Nursing home costs represent a relatively small portion of the average projected lifetime cost (24 percent, or $63,000), but these costs are also the primary driver of the significant variance: for the 95th percentile, nursing home costs represent 45 percent of the lifetime total, or $259,000. While these projected future costs decrease with age, they do so only marginally, as Figure 21.4 shows. The older someone is, the longer their life expectancy, and much of the lifetime costs occur at the end of life.

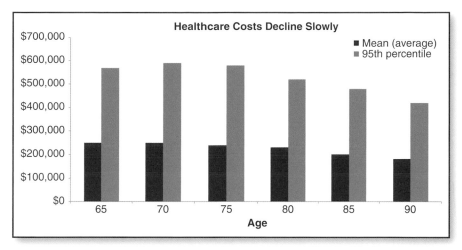

FIGURE 21.4   Mean and 95th Percentile of Remaining Lifetime Health-Care Costs Including Nursing Home Care, at Selected Ages
Source: Anthony Webb and Natalia Zhivan, "What Is the Distribution of Lifetime Health-care Costs from Age 65?," Chestnut Hill, MA: Center for Retirement Research at Boston College, 2010.

Long-Term Care Insurance

To eliminate some of the volatility (or risk) associated with these future health cost liabilities, the Family CFO can consider long-term care insurance. This insurance is designed to finance the costs incurred in chronic illnesses, including assistance with eating, bathing, and toileting. Care may be provided at home, a nursing home, or an assisted living facility. Approximately two-thirds of people 65 and over will eventually require some type of long-term care, including 20 percent who will need care for five years or more.

While Medicaid pays about 43 percent of all long-term care, to get it you have to exhaust almost all private resources first. Medicare covers only limited care, generally for a short period related to rehabilitation for a specific problem. In sum, it is highly likely that a 65-year-old couple will require some type of long-term care. This liability must be either self-insured or covered through a long-term care policy.

Recommendations of specific policies are beyond the scope of this book, but important selection criteria include the daily benefit amount, the elimination period (how long you have to wait before making a claim—similar to a deductible), the maximum benefit period, ability to pool the benefit with your spouse, inflation protection, and guaranteed right of renewal regardless of your health. Premiums vary greatly depending on both individual circumstances and policy terms. In 2010, however, the average annual cost for a policy with a 90-day waiting period, four to five years of lifetime benefits, a daily benefit of $150, and inflation protection was $2,261 for people between 55 and 64. Studies have shown that purchasers of long-term-care products generally recoup only 80 cents in benefits for every dollar of premium.

■ Key Conclusions

If you have the financial assets to assume these risks and potential liabilities, it's best to self-insure longevity risk and retirement health-care costs beyond those covered by Medicare. Purely as an investment, insurance is generally a bad choice and should be procured at the minimum levels needed to avoid financial distress. Those without the asset base to self-insure (most of America, given the significant financial burden that can result from the need for long-term care) should consider insuring these risks.

Annuities and long-term-care insurance should be considered together because the liabilities they insure are highly correlated. An annuity pays off the longer you live. Expected health-care costs also increase the longer you live.

Annuities are the more flexible and superior product because they provide a hedge not only for longevity but also for health-care costs. Furthermore, the pricing of annuities tends to be more attractive than that of long-term care products.

Many financial decisions such as investments in equities and the purchase of life insurance are most attractive when implemented early in life. For annuities, the opposite is true. I believe these products are most attractive when purchased very late in life. For example, by age 70 you have significant information regarding the status of your and your partner's health, the performance of your investments, and your benefits from Social Security. At this point, you can make an informed decision about the purchase of an annuity while also maximizing the bang for your buck: The payout on an annuity purchased late in life is much higher and maximizes the mortality credits.

What's Your Number? Determine When and How Much You Can Afford to Spend in Retirement

179

Uncertainty is a part of everyday life for all of us. Will it rain today? Will my car break down in the next 10,000 miles? How much will I make at my job this year? Next year? Will my spouse and I stay healthy? The questions cannot be answered with certainty. We know this, we accept it, and deal with the unknown as best we can. Unfortunately, when it comes to retirement, many of us are less accepting of uncertainty—we want to know *today* how much we can afford to spend for the rest of our lives! To get a sense of how ridiculous this expectation is, imagine asking your boss for a commitment today about how much you will make for the next 30 years. I suspect you'd be told it depends—on how you perform, how the company performs, the nature of the labor markets and inflation, and so forth. Bottom line: Your future salary will depend on a number of factors that can't be determined today. The same can be said about your retirement spending.

In this chapter, we explore frameworks for retirement planning, including ways to estimate your retirement income and manage your finances in retirement by adjusting your plans with the benefit of new information about your investment returns and your spending needs. These are good tools. But recognize that while the decision to retire must be made at a particular time with the information on hand, good retirement management happens continually throughout your retirement.

Approaching retirement, many people confront the question, "Can I afford to retire?" In other words, do I have enough money to fund my required consumption until death? In practice, the answer is a product of the actions, planning, and decisions you have made over a lifetime regarding your career, your consumption, your savings and, most important, when to retire. Given the magnitude of your retirement decision, it deserves some significant discussion and analysis.

This chapter gets into the how-to details of retirement planning: actually calculating how much you will need to save, how much risk you will need to take to hit your retirement spending goal, and more. If you are within several years of retirement, I suspect you will find this of great interest and happily study it numerous times to master the concepts to ensure a financially secure retirement. (To customize your retirement assumptions, use the tools at familyinc.com.) If you are still far away from this part of your financial journey, feel free to skip the rest of the chapter and come back in a couple of years.

■ The 4 Percent Withdrawal Rule

Perhaps the most quoted retirement planning rule of thumb is the 4 percent withdrawal rule, based on a 1998 paper by a group of professors at Trinity University in San Antonio, Texas. In its simplest form, this rule states that you can fund your retirement spending with minimal risk of running out of money if you withdraw 4 percent of your initial portfolio value annually, adjusted for inflation. This withdrawal rate was based on a generic portfolio consisting of 60 percent stocks and 40 percent bonds with a constant inflation-indexed withdrawal rate for 30 years. This plan has historically had a 90 percent chance of success (that is, nine out of 10 times the portfolio had a positive balance at the end of the 30 years). The probability of success is developed through the Monte Carlo simulation technique described in previous chapters or by using historic returns to back-test these scenarios. These simulations are fraught with assumptions, so the withdrawal rate you develop is not an answer but rather a starting point. It is subject to significant variation and risk, and can be modified over time with the benefit of actual investment returns and spending decisions.

Here are some of the assumptions that provide the foundation of the 4 percent rule:

- Future returns will have the same pattern as historical returns.

- All family members consuming these retirement assets have a life expectancy of less than 30 years from the date of retirement. (If you and your spouse retire at 45, this rule isn't for you.)

- You employ a traditional portfolio allocation of 60 percent equities and 40 percent fixed income, using a low-cost investment strategy that results in minimal drag from fees and taxes.

- Your priority is providing adequate consumption during your retirement rather than creating a legacy or inheritance. The proposed withdrawal rates are designed to maximize consumption in retirement while substantially exhausting the estate within 30 years.

It's worth looking at how the financial advisory community applies the 4 percent withdrawal rate to forecast the savings a family needs to retire. The numbers that follow are based on the Family Income Statement and Balance Sheet examples presented in Chapter 19. While those financial statements aren't those of a retiring couple, they are still instructive about the implications of a spending rule. These are the steps in applying the 4 percent rule:

Determine current after-tax consumption. The sample income statement shows that the family spends $7,200 per month or $86,400 a year.

Subtract estimated pension and Social Security income. This family has no anticipated pension but expects to receive monthly Social Security benefits for both husband and wife of approximately $2,000 each at age 67.

Determine income generated from investments using the 4 percent rule. Employing the 4 percent rule, the family's investments of $739,000 (excluding the primary residence) produce $29,600 of annual distributions. Adding anticipated annual Social Security payments results in approximately $77,600 of pre-tax income. Assuming an effective tax rate of 25 percent, this means the family projects $58,200 of after-tax cash flow to support consumption of $86,400—leaving an annual deficit of $28,200.

Find the required savings amount. This deficit can be addressed by spending less or by saving more. To address this shortfall entirely by accumulating additional savings, however, would require almost $940,000, which is the capital required to generate $28,000 after tax using the 4 percent rule. So this family probably needs to reduce planned retirement spending.

I advocate employing this type of analysis to establish a relationship between required savings and expected retirement consumption, but I recommend a very different approach to the generic 4 percent rule to align it more closely with real-world circumstances. Once again, the financial community in general has got it backward. For all of your working life, advisers design "customized" investment programs for you (for a fee) because they say your needs and risk tolerance are unique. When the subject comes to retirement, however, many apply the same 4 percent rule generically without acknowledging the unique circumstances of each retiree.

I take the exact opposite perspective. When considering asset allocation (managing investment risk), I argue that there is only one variable that should determine risk tolerance: the expected time horizon for liquidation. The longer the time horizon, the more equity exposure is appropriate. When retirement is at hand and you need to determine your withdrawal rate, you must also determine the minimum acceptable shortfall risk you are able to tolerate. Matters such as life expectancy, current health, overall wealth, fixed costs, and guaranteed income such as annuities and Social Security all dramatically affect a retiree's risk profile, which in turn affects the optimal withdrawal rate. This tension between consumption today and the risk of depleting your savings in the future is unique for every family on the basis of its circumstances.

Let's look at some real-world examples. My father officially "retired" at age 75, but still works part time. Both he and my mother collect Social Security and draw a pension. They have few debts or other fixed obligations, have purchased long-term-care insurance, and almost all of their consumption is funded by their pensions. My brother and I are both financially secure, so our parents have no need to plan for our financial needs. Dad's portfolio is equity rich. Contrast Dad's situation to my grandmother's. Grandma lost her husband when she was in her late fifties and retired early so she could move near her family. She supported herself with Social Security, a small teacher's pension, and some modest savings. As a survivor of the Great Depression, she invested much of those savings in government bonds. Her biggest asset was her house, which had a mortgage. Perhaps most important from her perspective, Grandma was an educated and proud woman determined to maintain her independence by living alone and not burdening her three daughters. Her own mother passed away at the ripe age of 97, and Grandma planned on doing the same in her own home.

Many financial advisers would likely recommend the same 4 percent withdrawal rate for these very different risk profiles. For Grandma, I would argue that the 4 percent rule (with its 10 percent probability of shortfall within 30 years) is too aggressive. In her late fifties, the probability of her living longer than 30 years was significant; she had significant fixed expenses relative to her income, and her investments were heavily tilted toward fixed income. Most important, the costs of a shortfall for her were significant—she would lose her independence.

For Mom and Dad, the 4 percent withdrawal rate is way too conservative. In or just beyond their seventies, their life expectancy is significantly less than 30 years. They have few debts and lots of guaranteed income to fund their current consumption and protect their quality of life should they deplete their savings. Dad likes to joke that he came into this world with nothing and intends to leave it the same way. I hope he lives up to his claim because it will mean he lived a long life and deprived himself of nothing he wanted and could afford. For Dad, the implications of exhausting his savings are of little consequence.

◾ First Determine Your Acceptable Shortfall Rate

As we demonstrated in our simulation analysis in Chapter 18, shortfall risk—the chance of running out of money during your retirement—is influenced by three things: (1) annual inflation-adjusted withdrawal rate, (2) portfolio composition, and (3) payout period. Figure 22.1 provides an estimate of the probability of shortfall for different scenarios given these three inputs.

Figure 22.1 can be used for developing recommendations that fit Dad and Grandma's unique circumstances. Dad's portfolio is equity heavy, averaging around 75 percent stocks and 25 percent bonds, and at age 77 he is focused on a 20-year payout period, which reasonably covers his and Mom's life expectancy. Figure 22.1 shows that with a 4 percent inflation-adjusted withdrawal rate, he essentially has zero risk of exhausting his savings. More likely, he will unnecessarily deprive himself. Dad's situation allows him to take substantial risk. It would certainly be justifiable for him to target a

The Chances of Running Short								
PAYOUT PERIODS	ANNUAL WITHDRAWAL RATES							
	3%	4%	5%	6%	7%	8%	9%	10%
100% Stocks								
15 Years	0%	0%	0%	6%	14%	24%	29%	36%
20 Years	0%	0%	8%	20%	28%	35%	48%	55%
25 Years	0%	0%	12%	25%	37%	50%	58%	67%
30 Years	0%	2%	20%	38%	45%	56%	67%	73%
75% Stocks / 25% Bonds								
15 Years	0%	0%	0%	3%	13%	23%	30%	44%
20 Years	0%	0%	5%	20%	28%	40%	51%	69%
25 Years	0%	0%	13%	30%	42%	58%	68%	80%
30 Years	0%	0%	18%	40%	55%	65%	87%	95%
50% Stocks / 50% Bonds								
15 Years	0%	0%	0%	1%	16%	29%	39%	56%
20 Years	0%	0%	6%	20%	37%	57%	69%	77%
25 Years	0%	0%	17%	40%	58%	77%	77%	92%
30 Years	0%	4%	33%	49%	78%	91%	100%	100%
25% Stocks / 75% Bonds								
15 Years	0%	0%	0%	1%	23%	41%	66%	66%
20 Years	0%	0%	18%	48%	74%	86%	91%	97%
25 Years	0%	5%	42%	68%	75%	85%	92%	93%
30 Years	0%	20%	69%	78%	93%	100%	100%	100%
100% Bonds								
15 Years	0%	0%	0%	19%	46%	63%	66%	73%
20 Years	0%	3%	35%	63%	71%	72%	83%	92%
25 Years	0%	38%	67%	77%	82%	92%	92%	98%
30 Years	16%	65%	78%	89%	98%	100%	100%	100%

	Choices related to Dad		Choices related to Grandma

FIGURE 22.1 Estimated Portfolio Failure Rates Based on Various Inflation-Adjusted Withdrawal Rates, Investment Allocations, and Payout Periods
Source: Simulation data from Philip L. Cooley, Carl M. Hubbard, and Daniel T. Walz, "Portfolio Success Rates: Where to Draw the Line," *Journal of Financial Planning* 24, no. 4 (April 2011).

failure rate of around 50 percent. Based on the figure, he could adopt a withdrawal rate of almost 9 percent—more than double the spending of the one-size-fits-all 4 percent rule.

Grandma, on the other hand, has an investment portfolio that is closer to 25 percent stocks and 75 percent bonds, and she has a 30-year-plus planning horizon. At a 4 percent withdrawal rate, her risk of failure is 20 percent. Given her circumstances, her acceptable failure rate should arguably be less than half that. Figure 22.1 allows her to understand the trade-offs between consumption, time, and portfolio mix. For example, to achieve her acceptable shortfall risk, Grandma can reduce her withdrawal rate to about 3.5 percent or change her portfolio to 50 percent stocks/50 percent bonds with a 4 percent withdrawal rate (and coincidentally a 4 percent risk of shortfall). Note that she actually reduces her risk of shortfall by embracing more equity exposure.

This type of analysis can also allow Grandma to evaluate the impact the retirement planning choices might have on her secondary priorities such as leaving an inheritance for her three daughters or supporting her favorite arts charity. Figure 22.2 uses the same inputs—inflation-adjusted withdrawal rate, portfolio mix, and payout period—but reports median end-of-period portfolio value rather than risk of shortfall. For example, if Grandma adopts a portfolio of 50 percent stocks and 50 percent bonds, with a 30-year payout and 4 percent inflation-adjusted withdrawal rate, this also leaves her with a median ending portfolio value of 297 percent of her initial portfolio. If Grandma started with $100,000 the most likely value of her portfolio in year 30 would be $297,000.

Be aware that the precision of these projections is illusory. Figure 22.1 shows failure rates based on back-testing returns of the S&P 500 and high-grade U.S. debt between 1926 and 2009. For these specific failure rates to apply to your plan, you must accept that the returns of those 83 years are representative of the returns you are likely to see during your withdrawal period. Even if you don't believe that, however, the general relationships between withdrawal rates, investment allocations, and payout periods are likely to remain. See familyinc.com to conduct your own withdrawal sensitivity analysis.

Building or Exhausting Your Estate								
PAYOUT PERIODS	**ANNUAL WITHDRAWAL RATES**							
	3%	4%	5%	6%	7%	8%	9%	10%
100% Stocks								
15 Years	383%	176%	301%	246%	202%	143%	86%	48%
20 Years	673%	581%	510%	342%	195%	122%	36%	0%
25 Years	871%	630%	510%	293%	168%	0%	0%	0%
30 Years	1293%	1008%	724%	413%	125%	0%	0%	0%
75% Stocks / 25% Bonds								
15 Years	314%	160%	216%	177%	129%	94%	61%	28%
20 Years	455%	373%	297%	205%	123%	45%	0%	0%
25 Years	598%	424%	288%	151%	38%	0%	0%	0%
30 Years	853%	597%	355%	134%	0%	0%	0%	0%
50% Stocks / 50% Bonds								
15 Years	232%	139%	154%	127%	89%	49%	18%	0%
20 Years	287%	226%	167%	107%	47%	0%	0%	0%
25 Years	373%	244%	145%	58%	0%	0%	0%	0%
30 Years	475%	297%	138%	1%	0%	0%	0%	0%
25% Stocks / 75% Bonds								
15 Years	160%	101%	78%	46%	6%	0%	0%	0%
20 Years	179%	120%	78%	27%	0%	0%	0%	0%
25 Years	185%	94%	7%	0%	0%	0%	0%	0%
30 Years	233%	63%	0%	0%	0%	0%	0%	0%
100% Bonds								
15 Years	133%	85%	61%	30%	5%	0%	0%	0%
20 Years	106%	62%	15%	0%	0%	0%	0%	0%
25 Years	92%	10%	0%	0%	0%	0%	0%	0%
30 Years	63%	0%	0%	0%	0%	0%	0%	0%
					Choices related to Grandma			

FIGURE 22.2 Median End-of-Period Portfolio Value (as a Percentage of Initial Portfolio) at Various Inflation-Adjusted Withdrawal Rates

Source: Simulation data from Philip L. Cooley, Carl M. Hubbard, and Daniel T. Walz, "Portfolio Success Rates: Where to Draw the Line," *Journal of Financial Planning 24, no. 4 (April 2011).*

Figure 22.2 reaffirms the benefits of long-term equity investing. It shows that if Grandma changed her portfolio allocation from 50 percent stocks/50 percent bonds to 100 percent stocks she would not only decrease her probable shortfall risk from 4 to 2 percent, but would also increase her expected ending portfolio value to 1,008 percent of the original value. These explosive increases in expected value highlight the importance of reviewing your finances in retirement to account for actual experience. If these increases began to materialize, Grandma could significantly increase her annual withdrawals even if, as we urge, she followed the asset allocation recommended in Chapter 16 and didn't actually put 100 percent of her portfolio into equities.

■ Identifying Your Withdrawal Rate

What should be your withdrawal rate? To know that, there are several steps to consider.

Determine your expected portfolio composition. If you follow the recommendations in this book, you will likely have equity exposure higher than 75 percent when you start retirement. So let's use a 75 percent stocks/25 percent bonds assumption for our retiring family.

Determine your expected payout period. I recommend using a mortality table to account for your age and marital status. The family in our example comprises two 67-year-olds in good health, so a 30-year payout period is a reasonable assumption.

Determine your acceptable risk of shortfall. Let's assume this family has a normal balance between maximizing consumption and leaving a legacy, so they have adopted a 20 percent shortfall risk as their acceptable threshold.

Approximate your withdrawal rate. With these inputs, you can zero in on your potential inflation-adjusted withdrawal rate from Figures 22.1 and 22.2. Our sample family's decisions put their preferred inflation-adjusted, after-fees withdrawal rate at 4.75 percent, which yields an expected failure rate near 18 percent and projects the ending value of their investments at around 350 percent of the value at retirement.

Now that you have determined a potential retirement withdrawal rate to meet your unique circumstances, several adjustments are required to ensure it reflects the reality of your finances. Significant items that don't persist through retirement, like the living expenses needed to defer taking Social Security until age 70 or the remaining payments on an old mortgage, are prefunded: In the sample retirement plan in Table 22.1, the forgone income or remaining payments are subtracted from assets listed on the balance

	Traditional 4 Percent Rule	Adjusted Withdrawal Rule
Investment Assets	$989,000	$989,000
Adjustments:		
Credit card debt		−$30,000
Value of home	−$250,000	−$250,000
Outstanding mortgage balance		−$200,000
Forgone Social Security		−$249,600
Anticipated health-care liability		
Adjusted Investment Assets	**$739,000**	**$259,400**
Deduct Investment Fees		
Standard 4 percent rule	4%	4%
Minimum safe shortfall adjustment (+/−)		1%
Allowance for investment fees		−0.25%
Adjusted Spending Rule	**4.00%**	**4.75%**
Deduct Taxes		
Annual investment income (Adjusted spending rule percent of adjusted investment assets)	$29,560	$12,322
Tax rate	25%	25%
After-Tax Investment Income	**$22,170**	**$9,241**
Add Social Security		
Retirement at 67	$48,000	
Retirement at 70		$62,400
Tax rate	25%	25%
After-Tax Social Security	**$36,000**	**$46,800**
Total Annual Income After Fees and Taxes	**$58,170**	**$56,041**
Annual Expenses	$86,400	$86,400
Adjustments		
Credit card payments		−$4,200
Mortgage payments		−$21,600
Long-term-care insurance		$5,000
Adjusted Annual Expenses	**$86,400**	**$65,600**
Annual Cash Flow Deficit		
Income minus expenses	−$28,230	−$9,559
Incremental Cash Flow Generated by Adjusted Withdrawal Rule		$18,671
Incremental Savings Required to Cover Annual Deficit	**$941,000**	**$268,319**

sheet, and the mortgage payments aren't included in annual expenses. The intention is that the finite number of payments will be made directly from investments without distorting long-term annual spending plans.

■ Modifications to Personalize Your Unique Withdrawal Rate

To home in on the right withdrawal rate for you, take account of these reminders.

You can't ignore debt, including:

- *Unsecured debt related to consumption.* This type of debt, mostly through credit cards, relates to past consumption and is the same as negative savings since the liability provides no ongoing benefit. Credit card debt should be deducted from your investment assets (or preferably paid off) with no corresponding decrease to the budget unless your budget included credit card payments.

- *Secured debt such as auto loans.* This debt should remain on the balance sheet and in the budget as a continuing expense, as the family will probably require a new vehicle as the current one ages and depreciates. If you don't intend to replace the asset associated with the debt, subtract the remaining debt from your investable assets while also subtracting the monthly payment from your projected expenses.

- *Mortgages.* Assuming you have followed the recommendations about managing your debt provided in Chapter 12, your after-tax, after-inflation cost of mortgage financing is unlikely to exceed your expected long-term real return on your investments, so it's prudent not to pay it off upon retirement. Your projected budget need not assume mortgage payments in perpetuity unless, unlike most retirees, your mortgage isn't fairly close to being paid off. If the payoff date isn't far off, you should exclude mortgage payments from your projected monthly consumption requirements in retirement while also subtracting your mortgage balance from your investment assets available to support your consumption.

In retirement, treat your home equity differently from other investment assets. Some families have accumulated significant wealth in their primary residence, making it a major part of their entire portfolio, and this asset can be considered in retirement planning. If you decide to include the home equity in your retirement planning, understand that you must be committed to tap into this equity either through a home equity loan, a reverse mortgage, or by selling your house at some point. If you expect to sell, commit to doing so relatively early in retirement so you don't find yourself overly dependent on this illiquid asset late in retirement after you have consumed your other assets. Practically, I find that most retirees who can afford to prefer to stay in their homes as long as their health allows and don't treat it as a pure investment asset. In this case, the home value should be deducted from investable assets because you are making a choice to exclude this from a planned liquidation.

You can't ignore likely contingent liabilities. The most obvious contingent liabilities for retirees are health-care costs, and they probably will be significant, based on the numbers highlighted in the previous chapter. Therefore, you should either include the cost of long-term-care and supplementary Medicare insurance in your budget or subtract the expected cost of these liabilities from your investment assets available for consumption.

You can't ignore fees. Because asset management fees can vary greatly by client and investment strategy, most studies ignore this expense, which can be substantial. I recommend deducting these fees and expenses from your withdrawal number. For example, if like our sample family, you planned on spending 5 percent a year but you have a weighted average expense burden on your investments of 0.25 percent, you should establish your budget on the basis of a 4.75 percent assumption.

You can't ignore Uncle Sam. Most retirement analyses assume that a retiree's tax bracket will be minimal. For many families, this is a reasonable assumption. If you are reading this book and create enough wealth that you can afford to consume $86,400 a year from your investments and Social Security benefits, however, you will likely pay more than minimum taxes. For planning purposes, our modified example assumes a conservative 25 percent effective tax rate for all sources of income, including Social Security, withdrawals from retirement accounts, and other investment income.

Defer starting Social Security payments to age 70. By doing so, you will have to use savings to replace these payments for three to four years (assuming retirement at 66 or 67). I therefore recommend including the higher anticipated Social Security payment based on age 70 in your consumption projection but subtracting the present value of that three- to four-year cash flow from your investment assets.

■ The Modified Percentage Withdrawal Calculation

These suggestions won't necessarily imply a more austere retirement. In our example, detailed in Table 22.1, they result in the following modified withdrawal calculation, which provides a better idea of how much money the family will need to generate from investments, given your minimum acceptable failure rate. Make the following adjustments.

Calculate your expected after-tax income from investments and pensions:

- Adjust investments to exclude (a) assets you don't plan on selling to support consumption, like your house (in our example, $250,000); (b) debts that won't recur, such as mortgages ($200,000) and credit cards ($30,000); (c) prefunded living expenses required to replace deferred Social Security payments until age 70; and (d) future liabilities such as health care if you plan to self-insure. (Our sample family chose to buy long-term-care insurance, which is reflected in their budget, not in an adjustment to assets.)

- Apply your personal spending rule adjusted for your risk tolerance and investment expenses (4.75 percent) and subtract taxes, assumed here to be 25 percent.

- Add your anticipated after-tax Social Security benefits. This represents the total after-tax income available for consumption of $56,000.

Determine your retirement consumption:

- Adjust annual expenses to reflect (a) remaining payments on debts that you have subtracted from your assets because they will soon be retired (in our example, $4,800 toward credit cards); (b) outstanding mortgage payments ($21,600); and (c) costs of insurance for items like long-term care if you haven't prefunded this cost in your balance sheet.

Compare the projected annual after-tax income of $56,000 to annual adjusted consumption of $65,600. The difference of $9,600 represents this family's annual deficit.

Calculate your implied required net savings—the amount you must have saved by retirement to offset the deficit and generate your needed income. In our example, the modified withdrawal formula results in more spending power than the standard 4 percent rule, and so, requires less additional savings. The modified rule, based on all the recommended changes to asset values and projected long-term expenses, results in adjusted net investment assets of about $259,000 with a withdrawal rate of 4.75 percent, yielding a first-year deficit of just $9,600—less than a third of the projected first-year deficit from the traditional 4 percent rule. With several years remaining until retirement, this deficit can be made up with appreciation and incremental savings of approximately $270,000.

In sum, the modified withdrawal rule results in a substantial increase in cash flow for the family. While not ready to retire, our sample family is well on their way.

■ Turbocharging Your Retirement Number

While the modified withdrawal rate can result in greater consumption with lower target savings, many families still have a difficult time accumulating enough net savings to support the consumption desired in retirement. Several techniques can be employed to increase consumption levels: delaying retirement, drawing down your home equity, changing the portfolio mix to generate higher expected returns, increasing spending early in retirement at the expense of later consumption, annuitizing a portion of your retirement savings, and accepting more risk of outliving your money. Here are some considerations for each of those approaches.

Delay retirement. This method of increasing spending during retirement is pretty straightforward. For every year you defer retirement, you provide another opportunity for your savings to accumulate and grow before liquidating them for consumption, and your remaining life expectancy decreases by another year. Delaying retirement from 67 to 70 not only increases your investable assets but also likely allows you to increase your withdrawal rate. Consider the net worth sensitivity analysis we conducted in Chapter 18. Assuming assets of approximately $567,000 at age 67, with a 5 percent real compound annual return and an additional three years of income, these assets grow to approximately $680,000. Applying our modified withdrawal rate of 4.75 percent results in an annual drawdown of about $32,300 versus the original drawdown of $26,900—an increase of 20 percent. The increase could be even higher with a shorter expected payout period and a higher withdrawal rate.

A note of caution is merited on this point. Extending your career if you reach retirement age without achieving your financial goals can be an effective solution. Seniors often encounter health problems late in their careers, however, and if they do lose their job, it is often more difficult to find a new one. This should be a contingency plan, not the primary plan.

Tap into your home equity. If you do include the value of this asset in your investments for calculating your withdrawal rate, you must develop a new withdrawal rate to reflect the likely return associated with this asset. Given the difficulty of assessing the value of a relatively illiquid private asset and the regional pricing dynamics of real estate, it's much harder to extrapolate withdrawal rates on the basis of historical performance. The approach outlined here, however, is a reasonable rule of thumb for drawing down this asset in your projected spending, with a low risk of shortfall.

- Determine the value of your residence through a real estate agent or independent appraisal.

- Calculate the expected proceeds from the sale of your home conservatively, since its actual value on the market in a future sale can't be known. Discount the appraised value by 20 percent as a cushion against transaction costs and an illiquidity penalty (when you do want to sell, the state of the market and the time needed to sell are unpredictable). Also deduct the remaining mortgage debt, which you will pay directly from your investment assets rather than from the amount determined by your spending rule.

- Calculate the annual inflation-adjusted withdrawal rate percentage. Divide 100 by the number of years in the planned payout period. Subtract 1 from the result to find the percentage of the expected proceeds of a home sale to add to your planned yearly withdrawals.

As a simplified example, if your home is appraised at $200,000 and you owe $90,000 and are planning on a 30-year payout period, the calculation is as follows:

Expected proceeds equal $200,000 minus 20 percent cushion ($160,000) minus $90,000 mortgage balance—$70,000. Your annual inflation-adjusted withdrawal rate for the home equals 100 divided by 30 (the years of the payout period)—3.33 percent, minus 1 percentage point, yielding a 2.33 percent withdrawal rate, which will support additional spending of about $1,631 (2.33 percent of $70,000) in the first year of retirement.

It should be noted that employing this approach will cause your liquid investment assets to deplete more quickly than the original withdrawal rate because you will spend the incremental $1,631 a year from your liquid investments before you actually sell the house. That's why, if you deploy this strategy, you shouldn't wait too long to convert this illiquid asset into liquid investments that you can sell as needed.

Modify the portfolio mix. The 4 percent withdrawal rate was based on a portfolio allocation of 60 percent equities and 40 percent fixed income. We established in Chapter 10 that equities offer a superior long-term real return with minimal increases in long-term volatility. We proposed in Chapter 16 an asset-allocation model that establishes a fixed income target based not on a percentage of the portfolio, but on a consumption target of three years of anticipated liquidations. Making those adjustments implies a portfolio for our sample family containing approximately 80 percent equities at the beginning of retirement, decreasing over time.

Plan to spend less late in retirement. The withdrawal analysis so far is based on constant inflation-adjusted consumption throughout retirement. While this is intellectually appealing, it is inconsistent with most retirees' consumption patterns. People have a tendency to spend less as they get older. Federal statistics show that average spending peaks at approximately $58,000 for the 45-to-54 age group and decreases by some 46 percent for households headed by those over 75. Various factors, including mortality, decrease the size of the average family over time, from a peak of 3.3 members in households headed by people 35 to 44 down to 1.6 members for households headed by those over 75. Fixed costs also often go down substantially. For example, in the sample budget in Chapter 18, approximately 50 percent of monthly expenditures were related to fixed costs such as mortgage payments, car loans, and student loans. In the later stages of retirement, many households retire these loans and don't replace them. Some 85 percent of homeowners over 75 have no mortgage. The one big exception to decreased spending later in life relates to health-care expenses, as discussed in Chapter 20.

Employ annuities to increase spending. Partially annuitizing your portfolio, as discussed in Chapter 20, can result in increased annual consumption relative to your withdrawal rule. For example, if a 60-year-old couple has a $1,000,000 portfolio, applying a 4 percent withdrawal rate would produce $40,000 in annual income. A 30-year inflation-adjusted annuity for that couple would yield an initial withdrawal rate of approximately 5.45 percent. Annuitizing 25 percent of the portfolio with the 30-year annuity would allow them to safely withdraw $43,600 (5.45 percent of $250,000 plus 4 percent of $750,000). While self-insurance is always the cheapest form of insurance, if you are trying to find ways to stretch your portfolio to meet your consumption needs, this technique can make sense.

Assume more risk of exhausting your assets. While assumptions vary among studies, most financial advisers recommend withdrawal rates that produce failure less than 10 percent of the time over a 30-year period. This conservative approach is considered appropriate, given the significant hardship associated with running out of money. Your goal, however, is not to fund consumption for 30 years; it's to fund consumption for your family throughout your life. If you and your spouse are the same age and retire at 65, the chance that either of you will be alive at age 95 (30 years from the date of retirement) is less than 18 percent. Therefore, the actual likelihood of the portfolio failing *and* you and your spouse being alive to care is substantially less than your target failure rate. There is no right answer regarding acceptable risk levels, but it's at least helpful to explicitly acknowledge the issues that can influence both your time horizon and your risk appetite. Some of the factors that can influence risk appetite are these: the percentage of your retirement consumption funded by Social Security, defined-benefit pension benefits or annuities; the quality of your health insurance; the composition of your retirement spending among fixed, variable, and discretionary expenses; and the factors that influence longevity, such as pre-existing health conditions, family longevity history, and whether your portfolio must support a retired couple or an individual. Perhaps the only silver lining of a shorter life expectancy is the decreased probability of exhausting your assets.

Adjust consumption based on actual information. The preceding suggestions attempt to develop spending rules based on consumption patterns and historical returns. It's convenient for retirement couples to have a specific number that they can comfortably spend. Over time, however, a retiree will garner valuable information about *actual* returns, which can be incorporated into consumption rules or withdrawal-decision rules.

Authors Jonathan T. Guyton and William Klinger developed five formal withdrawal-decision rules in an attempt to maximize withdrawal rates early in retirement while minimizing the probability of prematurely exhausting your assets.* Their simulation results reinforce the contention that high equity exposure is the most reliable way to increase success and preserve purchasing power. They found that dynamic decision rules based on actual investment returns can dramatically increase initial consumption rates (by as much as 60 percent with an 80/10/10 equity/fixed income/cash portfolio, with a 90 percent chance of success). Their adjustments were relatively frequent, averaging about one every three years, but were skewed toward increases in spending over decreases by three to one. Given what we have learned about the general behavior of spending patterns as families age, this

---

*Guyton and Klinger's *Portfolio Management Rule* provides an algorithm for liquidating assets and rebalancing the portfolio to maintain target allocations. The *Inflation Rule* provides withdrawal adjustments to preserve purchasing power throughout the forecasted duration of retirement. The *Capital Preservation Rule* provides a mechanism for reducing withdrawal rates when adverse circumstances result in an unacceptably high probability of shortfall. The *Prosperity Rule* provides a mechanism for increasing the withdrawal rate when positive investment performance produces greater than expected wealth. The *Withdrawal Rule* provides guidelines for establishing the initial withdrawal rate and modifying it over time using the Inflation, Capital Preservation, and Prosperity rules.

seems more than adequate to yield acceptable levels of consumption. The power of these observations is not based on the specific rules, but rather on the benefits of a systematic spending program that acknowledges the portfolio's investment results and adjusts consumption accordingly. The best strategy is to apply the modified withdrawal rule and review distribution assumptions every two or three years to incorporate your actual spending and investment returns.

A Number Is Just a Number

Before we leave this section on determining your withdrawal rate, it is important to put this number into context. Many families fixate on this single number as an indicator of their risk without testing the assumptions and appreciating the limitations. The withdrawal analysis is only as good as the assumptions regarding asset allocations, returns, and longevity. Furthermore, the context of the family circumstances is every bit as important as the number. These recommendations on withdrawal rate assume you have taken the actions recommended here to prepare your balance sheet for retirement as well including items such as deferring Social Security, evaluating annuities or setting aside capital for potential long-term care liabilities, and excluding the equity in your house from your investment assets. If you have prepared your balance sheet in this fashion, than you are prepared for the volatility that may come with a higher withdrawal rate and an equity-biased asset allocation. Your withdrawal number is just a small part of the overall retirement plan.

Managing Your Retirement Portfolio to Minimize Taxes

Throughout this book, we have developed an investment strategy to minimize the drag of tax leakage by employing these concepts: Make maximum contributions to tax-sheltered vehicles such as IRAs and 401(k)s to pay less tax and enjoy tax-free compounded growth; bias your portfolio toward equities, which are more tax efficient than bonds; employ a long-term, low-turnover strategy—taxes on stock gains are triggered only when you sell; hold substantially all your fixed income investments in tax-deferred accounts; and to the extent possible, execute all your rebalancing needs within your tax-deferred accounts or through new contributions.

With these principles, it's possible to eliminate tax leakage almost completely during the accumulation phase of your working years. As you enter retirement, however, tax deferral becomes more difficult because you must liquidate holdings, which will trigger tax liabilities. In addition to the preceding concepts, you should consider the following tax minimization strategies during retirement.

Don't start Social Security benefits until age 70. As mentioned earlier, these benefits get favorable tax treatment for most retirees.

Purchase annuities in a retirement account. If you buy annuities in addition to Social Security, do so in your retirement accounts. Because annuities are essentially insurance, their payout above principal is treated as income. By purchasing in a retirement account, you defer paying taxes on these payments until you actually withdraw money from your account. In a taxable account, the payments are taxed when they are made.

Exhaust taxable accounts before retirement accounts. This technique allows you to maintain more pre-tax capital at work for you for a longer time.

Exhaust taxable accounts in the order of their increasing effective tax rates. Harvest losses against gains and sell accounts that have the highest tax basis first; this allows you to first withdraw principal, which has no tax liability. This technique should minimize your effective tax rate at least for the first several years of retirement.

■ Using Debt to Defer or Minimize Your Tax Liability

Most financial advisers recommend dramatically reducing debt in preparation for retirement. In certain circumstances, I actually recommend the opposite. For many retirees, it makes sense to refinance the primary residence and take cash out. This can make sense under three conditions: (1) if refinancing won't result in a significant increase in your interest rate; (2) if the rate is 6 percent or less for a 30-year mortgage; and (3) if you have significant assets in taxable accounts with a low cost basis (their worth today is much more than what you paid) and therefore selling would result in paying taxes on a large gain.

The following simplified example demonstrates the potential benefits of employing debt. The family's investment portfolio has a value of

$1,000,000 and a cost basis of $250,000. Their home is worth $500,000, and they can refinance up to $400,000 at 4 percent interest with a 15-year amortization schedule. Their combined federal and state capital gains tax rate is 18 percent. They intend to liquidate approximately $87,000 in pre-tax assets annually to support $75,000 in after-tax consumption. They assume their investments will return 7 percent annually with inflation and fees of 2 percent—a 5 percent real return. Here's what happens over time.

Scenario I: Borrow nothing and increase the family's annual withdrawal rate with inflation. The $1,000,000 portfolio yields approximately $1,636,000 of cumulative withdrawals with an effective tax rate of 14 percent, resulting in after-tax cash flows of a little more than $1,400,000, and is exhausted in about 15 years.

Scenario II: Fund the family's first $400,000 in retirement spending through mortgage borrowings. The portfolio yields approximately $1,830,000 of withdrawals with an effective tax rate around 13 percent and is drawn down by consumption and mortgage payments to the outstanding mortgage balance in about 18 years. The advantage is twofold: Deducting mortgage interest limits taxes and the value of the portfolio compounds longer before triggering capital gains tax.

Expected outcome. The $400,000 mortgage provides an incremental $170,000, an increase of approximately 12 percent.

This leverage does create incremental risk for the family: The return on the portfolio might not match the cost of borrowings. But the risk is mitigated by several factors. A 5 percent real compounded return after fees, adjusted for this family's tax profile, is consistent with historical results. The hardest risk for retirees to hedge is inflation risk, and a long-term mortgage with interest fixed is a hedge against inflation. Your home value is likely to keep pace with inflation, so you are essentially inflating away this fixed obligation. For families that itemize their tax deductions, the deductibility of the mortgage interest over the years represents another source of value. Finally, in many circumstances, the approach in Scenario II actually reduces, rather than just deferring, taxes because it cuts the number of taxable sales of investments during retirement. Upon death, taxable capital gains disappear as the investment cost basis is reset to fair market value for most estates' tax purposes. This is a classic scenario in which those who can afford to assume incremental risk are well compensated for doing so, but it is likely inappropriate for those who intend to exhaust all or most of their assets throughout a lifetime.

■ Understanding What Inflation Does to Your Purchasing Power in Retirement

Early in life, the potential value of labor represents a significant portion of family net worth, so the family is relatively well insulated against inflation. The nominal value of the family's labor assets will increase to preserve real purchasing power. Retirees no longer possess this hedge. Most retirees (and financial advisers) are myopically worried about nominal market returns and annual volatility when in reality they should be worried about inflation and its impact on real purchasing power. Table 22.2 highlights the crushing effect that compounded inflation can have on purchasing power over long periods: If inflation trends repeat themselves, a person retiring today will require $2,693 in 30 years, and more than $7,000 in 45 years, to buy what $1,000 buys today.

The best ways to mitigate this erosion of purchasing power are to pick a profession that maximizes your working life so your labor assets will continue to appreciate with inflation, favor owning equities over fixed income and cash, ensure that any annuities are inflation indexed, and borrow long term at fixed rates only. Purchasing inflation-adjusted annuities and borrowing at long-term fixed rates may not turn out to be the best investment choices, but the planning certainty they provide is likely worth the potential lost benefit.

Retirees face slightly different inflation risks than those in the broader economy. The Bureau of Labor Statistics publishes a modified consumer price index called CPI-E that emphasizes goods and services purchased by

TABLE 22.2	The Disappearing Dollar		
Time Period	Number of Years	Dollars Needed at End to Equal $1,000 in 1939	Percentage of 1939 Purchasing Power
1939–1964	25	$2,207	45 percent
1939–1969	30	$2,693	37 percent
1939–1974	35	$3,300	30 percent
1939–1984	45	$7,236	14 percent
1939–1994	55	$10,414	10 percent
1939–2004	65	$13,164	8 percent
1939–2014	75	$16,648	6 percent

those over 62, and from 1982 to 2011, this inflation rate increased at about 3.1 percent a year versus 2.9 percent for the broader CPI. While this incremental deterioration in purchasing power is relatively small, the compounding effect can be significant over the life of a retiree.

■ Key Conclusions

As you exhaust your labor asset by retiring, you are left with fewer tools to correct deficits that might arise, so risks of shortfall must be actively managed.

The 4 percent rule is oversimplified. Your withdrawal rate should be based on your acceptable failure rate, which reflects your unique circumstances and temperament.

Even in retirement and regardless of your risk profile, you are still well served by adopting a portfolio heavily biased toward equities. This strategy generally produces lower risk of shortfall with a substantially higher expected ending value for your heirs and causes.

The Family CFO still has lots of flexibility by managing spending and hedging major risks such as longevity, health-care costs, and inflation.

When managing your financial plan, adjust spending periodically to match your evolving views of longevity and your actual returns on investments.

When managing competing risks between investment volatility and inflation, protect against inflation. Erosion of your purchasing power from inflation is the primary threat to your secure retirement.

Avoid the Rat Race—Change the Game by Changing the Rules

Economically, owning your own business is far superior to being an employee in a business. Beyond economics, it can open a better life for you, your family, and your legacy. Section VI can help you think ahead—far ahead—and act accordingly.

CHAPTER 23

Pay Yourself What You're Worth through Entrepreneurship

Creating a life of financial independence is highly achievable but requires starting early, lots of hard work, a sound investment program, planning, saving, and persistence. That's the primary message of this book. If you stay the course, you can create a very comfortable life. But on this path to achieving financial security, you face competition in both labor and financial markets that makes the journey more challenging.

In the labor market, as we have learned, we can increase our return through education, selecting the right types of jobs, and extending our working lives. Still, our income is significantly influenced by competition. Today, only 15 percent of U.S. households make more than $100,000. So probabilities suggest that the path to significant wealth is not through traditional employment alone.

Over the long run, the capital markets are also efficient and competitive, so even with a sound investment strategy, we should not plan for long-term net real portfolio returns in excess of 5 percent. Essentially, both labor and financial assets are commodities whose return is driven by demand and supply. That's why it's difficult to achieve higher returns than the market averages over the long run.

Now I'm going to share with you a way to cheat the system—by avoiding the commodity trap in both labor and capital markets. This is accomplished by combining your labor and your capital to become an entrepreneur and business owner. When people talk about entrepreneurship, they often think of recent history's greatest successes such as Bill Gates, Jeff Bezos, or the boys from Google. For most entrepreneurs, the magnitude of the business opportunity is much smaller—but so is the required capital and the risk of failure. Less capital and less risk of failure can result in a compelling risk-adjusted investment opportunity for the entrepreneur and Family Inc. In this discussion, don't think of Microsoft, Amazon, or Google. Think of a real estate brokerage business, a consulting business, financial advisory services, or maintenance services for an industry in your area. Businesses like that have several things in common: They leverage a specific skill set that can be developed while satisfying your responsibilities as an employee (in other words, learning on someone else's dime); they all require minimal capital to start; the primary assets are your skill, knowledge, and relationships; and they are all the kinds of businesses that can provide numerous exit options when you decide it's time to retire or transition out of working full time.

The economic model of owning your own business is far superior to being an employee in a business for several reasons:

- *Longer duration*. When you're an owner, the line between employment and ownership becomes less distinct. Many owners prolong their productive labor assets. In their later years, they remain involved in core aspects of the business in a less demanding role but still enjoy the benefits of employment combined with ownership.

- *Superior return on investment*. Because you're combining your unique labor talents with your capital, you're able to avoid the commoditized nature of capital returns. In Chapter 4, we determined that a key metric for assessing an attractive business is return on tangible invested capital. As an owner of a business that you are funding, this metric represents your cash-on-cash return on your investment year in and year out. We also noted that good service-oriented businesses often generate annual after-tax returns on invested capital in excess of 50 percent! Needless to say, generating 50 percent after-tax returns from investments in your business is significantly better than the expected long-term net real equity return of 5 percent.

I should note that a 50 percent return on tangible invested capital does not necessarily mean that the investor receives that cash flow each year. He or she receives that value by either taking the cash or reinvesting it back in the business to support growth in the ultimate value of the business.

- *Superior tax efficiency.* Owning your own business is much more tax efficient than being an employee. As an owner, your opportunity for tax deductions that reduce your effective tax rate is far greater, and while you are taxed on the profits of your company, you are not taxed on increases in the enterprise value until you exit. This effectively allows significant long-term, pre-tax compounding as the value of your business rises.

- *Superior exit opportunities.* Probably most important financially, owning your business provides an opportunity to sell it later in life. Your initial investment not only provides cash flows from profits during your ownership, but also provides an opportunity to capitalize the business's future earnings and sell the stock the same way you would sell a publicly traded stock.

Figure 23.1 is a template for your own business projections and an example of how the cumulative effects of these dynamics can drive return on an investment over 20 years.

The highlights of this business's plan can be summarized as follows:

- An initial investment of less than $300,000 is enough to fund the start-up costs of the business, including the owner's salary of $100,000, until the company becomes cash-flow positive.

- Thereafter the company is consistently profitable, with a 20 percent pre-tax profit margin and reinvestment equaling 10 percent of each year's growth in revenues.

- Over 20 years, the company grows modestly, resulting in approximately $3 million in revenue at the time the owner exits and an approximate sale price of $2.5 million (five times pre-tax profit).

A number of implicit assumptions in Figure 23.1 will certainly turn out to be incorrect. However, these assumptions are relatively conservative. Many entrepreneurs do much better, but even with these modest assumptions, the financial case for this choice is compelling, resulting in an after-tax real internal rate of return on investment (IRR) in excess of 24 percent and a multiple of capital invested of approximately 15. Both are

How Starting a Business Can Create Wealth

Assumptions

Salary	$100,000
Salary real growth	2.5%
Business reinvestment rate (as a % of revenue growth)	10%
Profit margin (excluding salary)	20%
Long-term real growth rate (after year 5)	7%
Effective tax rate	35%
Expected EBITDA exit multiple at sale	5.0
Effective capital gains tax rate	20%

Year	1	2	3	4	5	...10	...20
Revenue	$100,000	$250,000	$500,000	$750,000	$1,200,000	$1,683,062	$3,310,838
Profits after salary (pre-tax)	($80,000)	($52,500)	($5,062)	$42,311	$129,619	$211,726	$502,303
Income tax	$28,000	$18,375	$1,772	($14,809)	($45,367)	($74,104)	($175,806)
After-tax profits	($52,000)	($34,125)	($3,291)	$27,502	$84,252	$137,622	$326,497
Reinvested in business	$150,000	$15,000	$25,000	$25,000	$45,000	$11,011	$21,660
Distributions to owner	($202,000)	($49,125)	($28,291)	$2,502	$39,252	$126,611	$304,837
Proceeds from sale of business							$2,511,513
Capital gains tax on sale of business							($502,303)
After-tax proceeds of sale							$2,009,210
Cumulative cash flow from distributions and sale							$4,436,260

Investment Returns Assuming No Sale

IRR	22.5%
Total Investment (3-year negative cash flow)	($279,416)
Cumulative Cash Flows (Years 1–20)	$2,427,050
Multiple of Capital	9.7

Investment Returns Assuming Sale in Year 20

IRR	24.3%
Total Investment (3-year negative cash flow)	($279,416)
Cumulative Cash Flows (Years 1–20)	$4,436,260
Multiple of Capital	16.9

FIGURE 23.1 An Entrepreneur's Business Plan

far above what an investor can expect from the public markets. Comparing these outcomes with the assets an employee might expect to accumulate, being a business owner is the superior alternative so long you believe your chances of success are greater than 20 percent.* And that calculation does not include the real benefits of the opportunity to extend your career as an owner, an expected lower effective tax rate, and the significant upside if the business outperforms these assumptions. Perhaps most important, being your own boss can be a lot of fun.

Of course, a balanced assessment of entrepreneurship must also acknowledge negative aspects of this choice, of which there are two that merit discussion. Entrepreneurs must deal with (1) the risks of illiquidity associated with owning a private company and (2) also the portfolio concentration it causes (all or most of your eggs are in one basket). In my opinion, the positive benefits far outweigh these concerns.

▪ Key Conclusions

Both labor and capital assets are commodities. It's hard to achieve above-average, long-term results.

A way around these obstacles is to combine your labor and your capital to become an entrepreneur and business owner.

Forget Google. Most business opportunities are much smaller—but so are the required capital and the risk of failure.

---

*The 24.3 percent real return on investment of this business compares with 5 percent expected net real return on publicly traded equities. In terms of return expectations from the two alternatives, I would be indifferent when the probability of getting the higher return is about 20 percent (24.3 times 20 percent = 4.86 percent expected return).

CHAPTER 24

Jump-Start Your Heirs' Financial Security

A legacy desired by most families is to help fund the next generation's success by supporting their educational and business endeavors. That's why providing capital to support a legacy is important among the functions capital plays in Family Inc.

The basic Family Inc. Net Worth analysis illustrated in Chapter 1 is based on the assumption that at age 25, a person starts with significant labor assets and no financial assets. (See Figure 24.1.)

This profile can be dramatically altered through inheritance or gifting. Providing heirs with capital that can be invested early in their adult lives allows them to benefit from the effects of long-term compounding. This has huge positive implications for wealth creation. Figure 24.2 employs all of the same assumptions except that it includes the addition at age 25 of a $100,000 gift that is invested with a 5 percent real, after-tax, after-fee return.

As Figure 24.2 shows, thanks to the long-term compounding of the incremental $100,000, that gift grows to be approximately 65 percent of all the financial assets accumulated through savings and investment by age 65. Wisely managed, the gift dramatically reduces the risk of financial distress. The $100,000 gift grows to the point that returns from financial assets exceed consumption by the time the person stops working. As a result, net

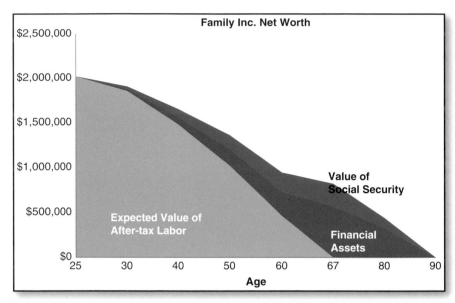

FIGURE 24.1 All Amounts = Constant Dollars

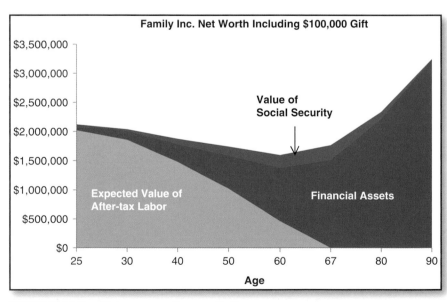

FIGURE 24.2 All Amounts = Constant Dollars

worth continues to grow even after labor assets are depleted. So with prudent consumption, the probability of outliving the assets becomes minuscule.

While Figure 24.2 assumes that nothing changes in the person's financial picture except the $100,000 gift, this is probably unrealistic. For better or for worse, the gift is likely to change behavior. It might negatively change the heirs' work patterns (they might work less) or consumption patterns (and spend more). While this is a possibility, I will focus on the positive benefit and leave the values teaching to the family.

Another important positive impact can be that this incremental financial asset allows the heirs both to pursue the magic math of entrepreneurship earlier and to embrace more volatile investments for higher long-term returns. For entrepreneurs to be successful, they must accumulate adequate experience and capital to support their future business endeavors. By providing capital, you can perhaps cut the time required for them to gain the experience to be successful business owners. As we discussed in the previous chapter, the after-tax return expectations of a business owner can far exceed those of the investment markets—by about 20 percentage points in our example. Let's say that at age 45, the heir invests the entire accumulated inheritance (approximately $225,000 by that time) in a business that results in a 24 percent compounded after-tax annual return through retirement at 65 (per our assumptions in the previous chapter) and also reinvests any distributions from the business back into the markets at a net real return of 5 percent.

As Figure 24.3 shows, the combination of the $100,000 gift with the opportunity to compound this capital at approximately 24 percent for a long time (45 years, in this case) dramatically changes the game.

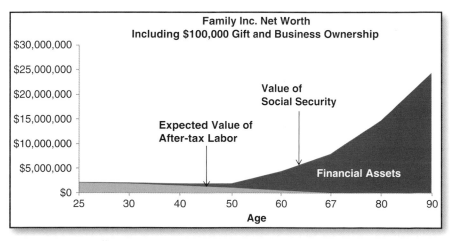

FIGURE 24.3 All Amounts = Constant Dollars

At age 65, this family has a net worth of almost $9,000,000, which will continue to rise as the asset growth far outpaces the rate of consumption.

In real life, business ownership up to age 90 and maintaining a 24 percent annual compounded return for that long are very unlikely. But even with a somewhat shorter holding period and lesser return, the growth in financial assets is compelling on a risk-adjusted basis.

■ Key Conclusion

If you have taught your next generation to be good stewards of capital, a financial gift, combined with hard work and prudent consumption, can generate exceptional levels of wealth for that generation and its successors.

CHAPTER 25

Develop a Succession Plan to Groom Your Replacement(s)

Dad has gotten a lot of things right when it comes to money—he saved well, invested well, managed his labor well, and ensured that his legacies (my brother and I) were well educated and capable of managing the family assets. In fact, because of Dad's mentorship, my brother and I have accumulated wealth that far surpasses his. Yet Dad has failed miserably when it comes to family succession planning. Although I've been professionally managing money for 20 years, he is unable to relinquish the leadership role when discussing family finances. He is unable to have a detailed accounting of his own financial circumstances or to promote an environment in which our extended family can openly discuss our financial situation, objectives, and ways to maximize these resources over multiple generations. Because of my father's rigidity in this area, I am sure that my family has missed out on valuable chances to learn from one another as well as on worthwhile estate planning opportunities. Dad is not alone: Most families miss this opportunity. The conversations can be daunting, delicate, and even embarrassing among family members.

Succession planning for the Family CFO is the most commonly neglected component of most family businesses, yet one of the most important actions that will determine the ability of Family Inc. to thrive over multiple generations. Many successful people work a lifetime to accumulate substantial wealth yet spend minimal time preparing their families to effectively manage this tremendous asset. When navigating this generational transition, it's helpful to look to corporate America for best practices. Among them are:

Leave your emotions at the door. One reason the discussion of generational wealth transfer is so neglected is that parents and kids often have a hard time interacting without the bias of family routine. When it comes to family financial business, the discussions and decisions should be based on the merits of the financial decisions, not the family roles.

Establish periodic strategic planning sessions to review Family Inc.'s performance. Just as a corporate board of directors meets to discuss the performance and strategy of a business, the Family CFO should orchestrate periodic meetings—at a minimum, annually—to review the status of Family Inc.'s performance over the preceding period, and any major initiatives over the coming period. This represents a low-stress way to engage and educate the family members about your finances.

Promote two-way communication. Parents often seem uncomfortable candidly sharing their financial situation with their children. This apprehension can be minimized in two ways. First, clearly establish that the family expenditures are at the discretion of the oldest generation—the parents should not feel guilty about consuming their accumulated assets and leaving less for the next generation, and the younger generation should not feel entitled to the assets of the parents. Second, promote a two-way exchange of information so that when finances are discussed, all family members are encouraged to share information and ideas, and to acknowledge shortcomings, mistakes, and weaknesses.

Establish that the skills necessary for the Family CFO require years to develop. Remember that your journey as a financially sophisticated professional has been an evolution. For most of us, it continues over a lifetime. Many of the concepts presented in this book are fairly complex. One of the primary responsibilities of the Family CFO is to be a teacher. Be patient and take every opportunity to teach and reinforce the lessons of financial security. It's difficult to start this education process too early.

Create opportunities for failure. Failure is a critical part of the learning process. We all have stories and experiences such as maxing out a credit card, failing at budgeting, committing financial infidelity (lying to your spouse about a purchase or how much something cost), or losing money on a stupid investment, and these experiences helped us become better financial managers, and maybe better spouses. As the Family CFO, you should create opportunities for your children to assume financial responsibility and likely fail. Give them access to a credit card, give them autonomy to spend budgeted money, give them authority to invest a small pool of capital. By doing this, you create valuable teaching opportunities and chances to fail with a relatively low cost. I would much rather have my kids learn the lessons of finance through small, controlled failures than catastrophically squander the family resources that I and previous generations of my family have spent working lifetimes accumulating.

Create financial incentives to promote engagement and participation. In business, we commonly fashion financial incentives to encourage desired behavior by employees and managers: pay raises, bonuses, and equity ownership. Financial incentives can also be effectively employed in managing and transitioning Family Inc. Common and effective financial incentives include the following.

- *Subsidized investments in labor development.* Encouraging highly educated heirs by subsidizing education is not only a great investment, but also a great way to perpetuate your extended family's financial success.

- *A matched savings program.* As many companies do with 401(k) retirement plans, you can promote higher savings rates among your children and their children by establishing a program to match all or part of what they save.

- *Compensation for responsibilities as a member of the Family Inc. board of directors.* Just as some companies pay for the services of an independent board of advisers, you might choose to compensate family members for actively engaging in family financial meetings and for specific financial management responsibilities such as assisting with tax preparation or managing rental property.

- *Capital contributions to heirs* based on enhancing desired Family Inc. performance metrics such as income or net worth. For example, one might make annual payments to family members based on a percentage of their earnings or net worth.

No technique is perfect. Those and many others, however, are all designed to have the same impact: promote responsible financial planning and behavior.

■ Key Conclusion

Allocate capital and bequests based on equity and fairness. Allocate control of financial resources and decisions on the basis of capabilities and merit. These two concepts don't necessarily go together. You can allocate your financial resources equally among heirs, but give disproportionate rights to heirs with the aptitude and personality to effectively manage, expand, and perpetuate Family Inc. Your heirs who are not financially astute may thank you in the long run for not simply awarding decision rights by default. Whether they thank you or not, they will be more financially secure.

CHAPTER 26

Develop and Manage Your Estate or Uncle Sam Will

217

A primary consideration of estate planning is to minimize taxes associ-ated with transferring assets to descendants. These taxes are significant for those who have accumulated significant wealth. In some cases, they can actually cause financial hardship to heirs if there's a large mismatch between the asset value transferred and the liquid assets available to pay the taxes—recipients can find themselves in the unfortunate situation of being asset rich but cash poor. For example, if you inherited real estate worth $10,000,000 but it is difficult to sell, you could have a tax bill in excess of $2,000,000 due 90 days from the date of death. A significant portion of inheritances is often illiquid, including assets such as family real estate or a family owned business.

Exemptions and tax rates for estate settlements have changed dramati-cally over time. Federal estate tax rates have ranged from zero to 50 percent and currently are up to 40 percent of transferred value after a $5,340,000 exclusion. Including state taxes can bring the effective tax bite well beyond 50 percent. Estate taxes actually affect few people but can be significant for those who meet the criteria. In 2013, only 0.14 percent of estates—1 in 700—are estimated to have paid taxes. For those who paid estate taxes in the past decade, however, the average tax liability was approximately $3,000,000, representing an effective tax rate between 14.7 and 21.8 percent. If you are reading this book, you either are or aspire to be one of the "unlucky lucky ones" who have to worry about estate taxes.

While minimizing tax liabilities is central to estate planning, other considerations are also critical, and some apply whether or not the estate is large enough to be taxed.

■ *Creating an effective will* so your wishes regarding the disposition of your personal affairs and assets are clear and not subject to dispute among potential recipients.

■ *Planning for the possibility of becoming disabled* and unable to take care of yourself, including designating who should make decisions on your behalf should you become incapacitated (often referred to as *designating a durable power of attorney*) and how end of life treatment should be administered (known as an *advance medical directive*).

■ *Developing a gifting strategy to minimize taxes.* This includes strategies to maximize the benefits of the so-called basic gift exclusion (you can give away up to $5,340,000 tax-free while alive or in your will); annual gift exclusions of $14,000 per recipient that don't count against the basic exclusion; and unlimited gifts for education and health care.

■ *Employing trusts* not only to transfer assets among generations tax efficiently, but also to provide rules for managing each trust and protecting the assets from creditors.

■ *Integrating insurance products into your estate plan* to provide quick cash to prevent the liquidity crunch for your descendants. Be sure the insurance proceeds will be paid outside the estate. You don't want that money to be taxed as part of the estate.

The specific tactics of executing an effective estate plan are beyond the scope of this book, given the complexity and constantly changing nature of the tax legislation. If you believe you are among the unlucky lucky whose heirs will be subject to estate tax, you absolutely need a financial adviser, an estate lawyer, or both. Developing an effective estate plan can be expensive, generally a minimum of several thousand dollars and often substantially higher. The cost depends on the size and complexity of your estate and requires frequent review and updates to accommodate your changing situation. Anyone who consistently earns more than $300,000 a year and expects to have net worth in excess of $5,000,000 should actively consider making this investment.

■ Key Conclusions

Few families actually pay estate taxes, but for those who do, the impact can be enormous. You may be among them, later if not now.

Some elements of estate planning apply to families at any income level.

Develop an estate plan now. Life is uncertain.

CHAPTER 27

Maximize Your Charitable Legacy

For most people who can, the most logical time to make major gifts to charity is late in life.

We established in Chapter 1 that legacy management is a distant third priority for Family Inc. after providing for the family's consumption and investing to build net worth for retirement. Unless you have been fortunate enough to accumulate significant wealth early in life, those goals are likely to take decades to accomplish.

We have discussed the many uncertainties a family faces. Late in life many of the answers are known—How good were my investment returns? How good is my health and how much longer do my spouse and I expect to live? Do we require long-term care? Are the kids healthy and financially secure? With the benefit of clarity on such critical issues, older families can make better-informed decisions about their need for contingency capital.

Furthermore, if you follow the investment guidelines offered in this book—indexing with low fees, low taxes, and high equity exposure—your investment returns are likely to be better than those of many of the charities you choose to support. Charities generally have to take low risks in their investment portfolios, partly because they may have a relatively short time horizon for needing the money and partly because persuading donors to support the cause is doubly challenging if there has been a history of investment losses.

In sum, by giving significant gifts later in life, you can do so with lower financial risk to the family and probably greater purchasing power for the charity than if it had managed the money itself. While your charity might not agree, later in life is generally a win-win for all involved.

Note that I am not suggesting that you withhold all giving until you are old. Throughout our lives, most of us give money and time to our favorite charities and community programs. This activity can be rewarding and is an important part of being a good member of your community and a decent human being. This chapter doesn't address this kind of normal course of giving, but rather focuses on large commitments likely to be made in the context of a long-term financial plan.

■ How to Select Worthy Charities

Many Family Inc. principles regarding investment selection also apply to charity selection, with some modifications.

- *Invest in what you know.* The world of charitable giving may be even more complex, more nuanced, and more perplexing than the financial landscape when it comes to identifying best-in-class nonprofit organizations. Disclosures are less robust and the performance metrics are less clear. For this reason, I recommend supporting organizations whose mandate you know something about. For example, the majority of my charitable giving goes to veterans' causes. In giving to these causes, I can leverage my knowledge and network to ensure my dollars are going to good use.

- *Clearly define your "giving" risk tolerance.* Just as an investor's risk profile influences asset selection, risk profile also influences charity selection. Are you looking for breakthrough moonshot-like outcomes from your charitable giving or are you looking for predictable, tangible, incremental positive outcomes for your cause? There is no right answer here except to say that if your risk profile is not aligned with the charitable organization's, it is sure to be an unsatisfying relationship.

- *Consult third-party resources to vet your charity.* Because charities don't pay income taxes, they are required to file annual IRS 990 Forms, available at irs.gov. These forms are a great place to start to get a clear sense of the organization's finances. Numerous other resources, such as Guidestar, provide independent evaluations, both free and paid, on topics like charities' governance, transparency, and executive compensation.

- *Demand clear metrics of performance.* In our investment program, once we define the right metric—long-term returns after taxes, fees, and inflation—evaluating performance is fairly easy. In the world of nonprofits, measurements of performance are harder to evaluate and can differ across organizations. How does a veterans' charity measure and evaluate itself on achieving its mission? Beware of any organization that is not actively measuring its performance and delivering quantifiable performance metrics. Without these metrics to serve as a road map for accountability, you have no way of assessing performance for your hard-earned investment dollars.

- *Beware of leakage that saps the impact of giving.* Just as expenses and fees can sap your investment returns, overhead that diverts your dollars from program expenditures diminishes the impact of your giving. Mature charities (not startups) should generally limit overhead expenses to less than 25 percent of total revenues.

■ How to Give

Effective giving takes more than writing checks. Here are some guidelines.

- *Build a portfolio of charity relationships.* In the same way that investors seek to create a diversified portfolio, I recommend nurturing relationships with several charities of interest. I'm not advocating (or discouraging) diversification among causes. For example, I support numerous charities, including several related to veterans' causes. This portfolio of relationships provides me with a more robust information network, allowing me to become more knowledgeable about my cause. It provides multiple opportunities to evaluate different organizations and discover the best practices, best management teams, and most successful models in my area of interest. Creating a charity portfolio is a key tool to becoming a value-added donor.

- *Stage your commitments.* Many donors adopt the "go big or go home" strategy of giving—they make one large gift to their charity and that's it. In my view, this is a bit like getting married without dating. I recommend staging your commitments over time to allow you to watch the organization perform as a steward of your capital. If they perform well, you can allocate more to them. This approach is especially helpful when you create a charity portfolio because it allows you, over time, to back your winners on the basis of their performance.

■ *Consider taxes.* As in investing, taxes matter when evaluating charities. When creating a giving plan, three key concepts are worth remembering: (1) Give away assets, not cash—this allows you to avoid the tax liability that would have been triggered upon your sale of the asset; (2) Give away the assets that possess the highest tax liability (lowest cost basis) first; (3) If you can, make your charitable contributions while you're alive; it generally saves taxes to do so rather than through an estate plan. To the extent that you are contemplating a sizable gift to charity, seek professional tax counsel. The rules are complex and the stakes are high.

■ *Combine your charity with your labor capital.* Chapter 23 highlighted the significant benefits of combining your labor with your capital through entrepreneurship. The same holds true for charity. The best way to maximize impact is to combine your capital donations with your labor contributions. Find a charity that has the positive attributes outlined in this chapter and also can benefit from your active participation. Not only will this have a multiplier effect on your contribution, but it will also improve your skills as a strategic giver.

■ Key Conclusions

In the late stages of life, many families accumulate enough wealth and gain enough visibility into their financial security to consider meaningful gifts to charity.

Apply the rules of Family Inc. asset management and entrepreneurship to maximize the impact of your gift.

A CALL TO ACTION

CHAPTER 28

"But It's Different This Time. . . ."

Throughout this book, we frequently rely on history to inform our views about the future. Meaningful recommendations about your education choices, your investment choices, your insurance needs, your investment program, and your retirement planning all draw on historical results to validate these recommendations. Some of the best minds in finance today, however, think that the future is unlikely to be as hospitable in the twenty-first century as it has been in the past. Some common concerns that could have a negative impact on our assumptions include:

■ The returns of U.S. equities over the past two centuries have been higher than in the rest of the world, reflecting tremendous economic growth unlikely be replicated in our mature economy.

■ International markets are facing strong headwinds. Developed Europe is overleveraged, and servicing this debt will rob future economic growth and development. Emerging markets are rapidly maturing. Their historical growth rates are unsustainable.

■ Global interest rates are at unsustainable lows. Normalization of interest rates will unavoidably create a drag on returns for all asset classes.

■ Governments around the world seem dysfunctional, and future generations will likely be faced for decades to come with the ongoing tax of fighting terrorism.

- Global population growth and aging, the depletion of scarce resources, and the costs that development extracts from the environment are all likely to hinder future growth.

Among all these concerns, the bar for achieving financial security is ever rising as people live longer, the costs of education and health care continue to increase much faster than inflation, and the safety net traditionally offered by employers and the government continues to fray.

Does this pessimistic view of the world invalidate our recommendations? The genius of this book is that no matter what the future holds, the recommendations offered throughout remain valid—with one possible exception: the advice about retirement. No matter what the future holds, you are best served by sticking to these recommendations until you are within sight of retirement. When it comes time to manage your assets in retirement, you can adjust your withdrawal and investment strategies to reflect the realities of that time. If the future has been kind, you will likely retire in comfort with significant assets left over for your legacy. If the future has been unkind, you will have made the best of a challenging environment and will have employed techniques to mitigate the challenges presented by the markets: working longer, for example, and deferring Social Security and complementing your investments with annuities and long-term-care insurance. The odds that you will have the peace of mind and confidence to adopt a withdrawal rate that satisfies your desired lifestyle are on your side.

■ Key Conclusions

Throughout the financial game of life, we are forced to make all kinds of forecasts and estimates—about the financial implications of career choices, costs of education, investment returns, life expectancy, and inflation, to name a few. They will all be off base; get over it. This book gives you the tools to identify assumptions, make reasonable guesses on the basis of history, and course-correct along the way with additional information.

We can't predict the future, but we can adopt a strategy for all seasons.

CHAPTER 29

Put Down the Book—Just Do It!

Incorporating all that you've learned into the management of Family Inc. can be daunting. It's easy to experience paralysis by analysis. My advice to you: *Just do it!* You will make mistakes, absolutely, but the concepts of Family Inc. will keep you on course and help you self-correct as you develop your skills as a financial manager. If you sometimes feel lost in the details, remember the big-picture principles summarized here to guide your decisions in conjunction with your own common sense.

Don't think of yourself as an employee. You are an owner of Family Inc. Act accordingly.

You can't afford not to make investments in education. Favor schooling that allows you to maximize your chances of being competitive in the labor market of your chosen profession and your ability to work as long as you want.

Successful careers don't just happen; they must be managed. If you start out working for somebody else, simply being a good employee is only part of your business mandate. You must take responsibility for your career progression and choices—no one else will.

The principles of investing can guide you in allocating your labor assets toward work with the highest expected financial return.

Job number one of your asset management business is to provide liquidity for contingencies and to support your labor business and your consumption in difficult times. Always maintain an adequate reserve to meet this need.

When allocating your assets, be sure to include all components of Family Net Worth, such as labor, Social Security, and real estate.

Make reasonable assumptions for asset-class returns (equity returns of 4 to 5 percent after inflation, for example), and construct a portfolio heavily biased toward global equities through low-cost ETFs or tax-managed mutual funds.

When markets tremble, stay the course and remember the following investment truths: Successful investors maintain a long-term focus; over time, the performance of asset classes and managers tends to demonstrate reversion to the mean; shortfall and inflation risks are generally more damaging to financial independence than short-term volatility.

Actively track and monitor your family financial statements to ensure adherence to your plan and to check that your income statement, balance sheet, and liquidity stay managed in a fashion consistent with your risk tolerance and labor and consumption patterns.

Pursue entrepreneurship as a way to achieve higher financial returns for both your labor and capital. By redefining the traditional employer-employee relationship through entrepreneurship, you can avoid the commodity trap.

Actively monitor your shortfall risk—the chance that you're not on track to reach your goals. Manage your career and finances to mitigate this risk.

Maximize and perpetuate the value of your family legacy by actively teaching these lessons, gifting to fund the next generation's asset management business, and estate planning.

■ The Real Prize

They say money can't buy happiness and I certainly agree. However, the lack of it sure can make life challenging. My goal for this book is not to have you think about the financial impact of every decision you make, but rather to help you identify the big decisions and their implications in your financial life so you don't have to dwell on money every day.

In my personal journey to financial independence, money has become less important to me, not more, as I have accumulated wealth. Imagine a life where you live well within your means so you don't have to worry about every dollar you spend—if you really want or need something, you buy it. Imagine the peace of mind and comfort you get from knowing that you can send your kids to college, live comfortably in retirement, and handle the costs if you or your partner need long-term care.

Family Inc. is not intended to make you a slave to your financial goals. As they have done for my family, the principles here will help you achieve your financial goals—and free you to focus on the important things in life such as your family, loved ones, and professional and personal aspirations. Financial independence should not be your goal, but rather the vehicle to allow you to realize your passions, your potential, and your dreams.

How to Calculate Expected Lifetime Labor Value

231

Anybody's potential income from a lifetime of productively deployed labor is an asset that generates a stream of income and can be valued like any other financial asset. The financial instrument that the income stream from a person's labor most closely resembles is called a *present value growing annuity*.* An annuity is simply a financial contract that provides the owner with a periodic payment similar to annual interest payments you might receive by owning a bond, the primary difference being that when an annuity ends, there is no return of principal. Also different from a bond or a fixed annuity, most professionals experience an increase in their real earnings as they age and develop skills and experience. That's why your labor most closely resembles a growing annuity. By applying the growing-annuity formula to the stream of cash flows generated over a career, we can develop a formula for the expected present value of future labor. It looks like this:

Present value = (current after-tax annual compensation /

(inflation rate − growth rate)) × [1 − ((1+growth)/(1+inflation)) ^ n]

---

*A present value growing annuity is a finite series of cash flows that grows over time and is discounted to a present value based on anticipated inflation and the timing and risk of the cash flows.

In practice, what the formula does is sum up all future anticipated payments, reflecting that the payments grow over time but decreasing the value for the impact that inflation has on your future purchasing power.

A real-world scenario is perhaps the most effective way to show the practical application of this formula. Let's revisit the assumptions we used for determining a 25-year-old's Family Inc. Net Worth in Chapter 1.

- Current age: 25

- Retirement age: 67

- Current annual after-tax compensation (starting salary): $31,150*

- Annual growth rate of pay: 3 percent

- Assumed annual rate of inflation: 1 percent

Applying the growing-annuity formula to these assumptions regarding this worker's labor allows us to estimate the expected present value of his labor as follows:

$$(\$31,150/(.01-.03)) \times [1-((1+.03)/(1+.01))^{\wedge}42] = \$1,991,400$$

That result, approximately $2,000,000, should sound familiar. It's the same number we developed for his Family Net Worth when his only asset was labor.

---

*Based on $44,500 in pre-tax salary, assuming a combined effective income tax and Social Security tax rate of 30 percent. Starting salary approximates median annual earnings of someone with a professional degree.

alpha The difference between a manager's performance and the average performance of other managers, adjusted for the riskiness of the holding.

balance sheet A listing of all assets, liabilities (debts), and **net worth**. For the balance sheet to balance, assets must equal liabilities plus net worth.

fee leakage Shrinkage of the **gross return** on an investment because of management fees and other expenses.

free cash flow to equity A metric of how much cash can be paid to the equity shareholders after all cash expenses, taxes, reinvestments, and net borrowings.

gross return The total return on an investment before deducting any fees or expenses.

illiquid A security or other asset, such as real estate, that may not easily be sold for cash without a substantial loss of value.

impairment Permanent loss of all or part of original capital.

income statement Revenues (or salary/earnings) minus expenses equals profit or savings. In business, also known as a profit and loss statement, or P&L.

internal rate of return (IRR) The effective yield or compounded annual rate of return on an investment.

labor asset The **present value** of expected future after-tax income from working.

233

Monte Carlo simulation   A simulation technique used to demonstrate the range of possible outcomes given an expected outcome (mean) and the volatility of that outcome (**standard deviation**) by generating multiple trial runs.

near–cash   Very liquid assets including pocket cash, checking and money-market accounts, certificates of deposit (CDs), and Treasury bills.

net asset value (NAV)   The value of a mutual fund, calculated daily by deducting the fund's liabilities from the market value of all its shares and then dividing by the number of issued shares.

net worth   Financial net worth is the difference between assets and liabilities (the traditional definition of net worth). Financial earning net worth excludes all assets or durable purchases that lose value, or depreciate, with normal age and use. Family Inc. net worth includes **labor assets** and expected Social Security benefits as assets.

nominal   Not adjusted for inflation. Contrasts with **real**.

present value   A future amount of money that has been discounted to reflect its current value.

price-to-earnings ratio (P/E)   The market price of a stock divided by the company's annual earnings per share, a ratio for valuing the stock.

real   Adjusted for inflation. Contrasts with **nominal**.

return on assets (ROA)   The percentage of profit (net income) a company earns in relation to all the assets employed in the business.

return on equity (ROE)   The percentage of profit (net income) a company earns in relation to each dollar of common shareholders' equity (the company's net worth, or assets minus liabilities).

return on invested capital (ROIC)   The percentage of profit (net income) a company earns in relation to all the capital provided by shareholders and bondholders.

return on tangible invested capital (ROTIC)   The purest measure of capital efficiency, showing the percentage of earnings before interest, taxes, and amortization in relation to tangible assets minus cash and current operating liabilities. Tangible assets exclude nonphysical assets, such as patents, trademarks, copyrights, good-will, and brand recognition.

sensitivity analysis　A technique to determine how projected performance is affected by changes in the assumptions that those projections are based on. Also known as "what-if analysis."

standard deviation　A measure of risk or volatility, showing how broad is the dispersion of prices or other values around the mean (average). Most markets show "normal" distributions of prices—the familiar bell curve. In a normal distribution, the area of one standard deviation around each side of the mean represents 68.2 percent of all the recorded values. For example, the average of annual **nominal** returns on stocks has been 8.4 percent, and there is a 68.2 percent chance that in any year the returns will be within 18.1 percentage points (plus or minus) of 8.4 percent—one standard deviation. In other words, if you own equities, you have approximately a two-thirds chance that your return in any year will be within −9.7 and +26.5 percent.

tax leakage　Shrinkage of the **gross return** on an investment because of taxes on the gains.

volatility　A measure of how widely the price of a security or a market fluctuates, measured by calculating the **standard deviation** of the annualized returns over a period of time.

Chapter 1

health care and education costs have increased   U.S. Bureau of Labor Statistics, 2001–2011.

610 million credit cards   Federal Reserve, "Survey of Consumer Payment Choice," Boston, January 2010.

In 1970, there were approximately 360 mutual funds   Matthew Fink, *The Rise of Mutual Funds* (New York: Oxford University Press, 2008).

Chapter 3

The value of a stock option   This widely used method of calculating the value of an option is known as the Black-Scholes model.

Chapter 5

failed despite federal regulations   The regulations are in the Employee Retirement and Income Security Act of 1974 (ERISA).

■ Chapter 6

25 percent of today's 20-year-olds will become disabled   www.disabilitycanhappen.org/chances_disability/disability_stats.asp;   http://well.blogs.nytimes.com/2009/06/04/medical-bills-cause-most-bankruptcies/.

■ Chapter 8

smaller drops in many other types of assets   John Lovito and Federico Zamora, "Investment Viewpoints," Currency Management Series, American Century Investments, May 2010.

reduced volatility by more than 40 percent   Elroy Dimson, Paul Marsh, and Mike Staunton, *Triumph of the Optimists* (Princeton, NJ: Princeton University Press, 2002), 118. The global portfolio was "market-capitalization weighted." That is, securities are included in proportion to their market capitalization (price times number of shares outstanding), so larger countries and companies compose a higher percentage of the portfolio.

Evidence is scarce that these models are predictive   A study conducted by Vanguard concluded that tactical asset-allocation models outperformed the broader market by only .03 percent per month, before expenses, with little statistical significance (meaning that the outcome might have resulted from chance).

the 10 best and worst days represented   Ellen Rinaldi, "Market-Timing and Performance Chasing Are Losing Strategies," *Vanguard's Investment Philosophy:We Believe* 8 (2005): 3.

little real house price appreciation   Wei Sun, Robert Triest, and Anthony Webb, "Optimal Retirement Asset Decumulation Strategies: Impact of Housing Wealth," Federal Reserve Bank of Boston, 2007.

■ Chapter 10

the average real returns of 19 countries   Jeremy J. Siegel, *Stocks for the Long Run,* 5th ed. (New York: McGraw-Hill, 2014), 90. The analysis is based on data from Elroy Dimson, Paul Marsh, and

Mike Staunton, *Triumph of the Optimists: 101 Years of Global Investment Returns* (Princeton, NJ: Princeton University Press, 2002), updated through 2012.

One study analyzed the range of annual gains and losses   Ibbotson Associates and Vanguard Investment Counseling and Research.

◼ Chapter 11

Annual inflation has averaged   Donald G. Bennyhoff, "Preserving a Portfolio's Real Value: Is There an Optimal Strategy?," Vanguard Investment Counseling & Research, 2009, 3.

average real returns of stocks and government bonds exceeded   Ibid., 7.

◼ Chapter 12

After taxes, these returns drop to   Based on maximum annual tax rates applied from 1802 to 2006.

Over the life of the mortgage, this represents significant value   My example differentiates between returns on capital and cash flow. Because a 30-year mortgage or any loan is amortized, the cash flow will differ from my example. The value of the spread goes down over time because the loan balance goes down. This doesn't change the decision.

◼ Chapter 13

At the end of 2013, ETFs held   Murray Coleman, "ETFs Gain Ground on Index Mutual Funds," *Wall Street Journal*, February 20, 2014.

actively managed funds underperformed the benchmark   Jeremy J. Siegel, *Stocks for the Long Run*, 5th ed. (New York: McGraw-Hill, 2014), 359.

One extended study found   *Pioneering Portfolio Management*, 77. Data for marketable securities are from the Piper Managed Accounts Report of December 31, 1997. The data for real estate are from Institutional Property Consultants. The venture capital and leveraged buyout data are from Venture Economics. Venture capital and leveraged buyout data represent returns on funds formed between 1988 and 1993, excluding more recent funds so that immature investments will not influence reported results.

▣ Chapter 14

the economies of emerging market countries grew   Joseph H. Davis, Roger Aliaga-Díaz, C. William Cole, and Julieann Shanahan, "Investing in Emerging Markets: Evaluating the Allure of Rapid Economic Growth," Vanguard Research, April 2010, 3.

▣ Chapter 15

One study of data over 20 years   Scott J. Donaldson and Frank J. Ambrosio, "Portfolio Construction for Taxable Investors," Vanguard Investment Counseling & Research, 2007, 21.

▣ Chapter 21

Mortality   credits   www.annuitydigest.com/mortality-credit/ definition

annual payment of $62,000   *Annuity Shopper Buyer's Guide*, Fall 2015.

average uninsured health-care costs   *Healthcare Expenses and Retirement Income: How Escalating Costs Impact Retirement Savings*, January 2012, 3, IRIonline.org.

The present value of a 65-year-old couple's lifetime uninsured health-care costs   Anthony Webb and Natalia Zhivan, "What Is the Distribution of Lifetime Healthcare Costs from Age 65?," Center for Retirement Research at Boston College IB#10-4 (February 2010), 1.

two-thirds of people 65 and over will eventually require some type of long-term care   Peter Kemper, Harriet

L. Komisar, and Lisa Alecxith, "Long-Term Care Over an Uncertain Future: What Can Current Retirees Expect?," *Inquiry* 42 (Winter 2005/2006), Excellus Health Plan, Inc., www.inquiryjournal .org, 342.

the average annual cost for a policy "Long-Term Care Insurance," AARP Fact Sheet 261, 2012.

80 cents in benefits for every dollar of premium Howard Gleckman, "The Role of Private Insurance in Financing Long Term Care," Center for Retirement Research at Boston College 7–13 (September 2007).

■ Chapter 22

90 percent chance of success Geoff Considine, "Safe Portfolio Withdrawal Rates: Beyond the 4% Solution," November 28, 2006, seekingalpha.com.

Figure 22.1 "Portfolio Success Rates: Where to Draw the Line" www.onefpa.org/journal/Pages/Portfolio%20Success%20Rates%20Where%20to%20Draw%20the%20Line.aspx. Data for stock returns are monthly total returns to the Standard & Poor's 500 index, and bond returns are total monthly returns to high-grade corporate bonds. Both sets of returns data are from January 1926 through December 2009 as published in the 2010 Ibbotson SBBI Classic Yearbook by Morningstar. Inflation adjustments were calculated using annual values of the CPI-U as published by the U.S. Bureau of Labor Statistics at www.bis.gov.

Federal statistics show U.S. Bureau of Labor Statistics, 2010.

85 percent of homeowners over 75 have no mortgage Ibid.

developed five formal withdrawal-decision rules Jonathan T. Guyon and William Klinger, "Decision Rules and Maximum Initial Withdrawal Rates," *Journal of Financial Planning* (March 2006): 50–58.

inflation rate has increased at about 3.1 percent versus 2.9 percent "Focus on Prices and Spending," U.S. Bureau of Labor Statistics 2, no. 15 (February 2012).

▪ Chapter 26

Only 0.14 percent of estates   Chye-Ching Huang and Nathaniel Frentz, "Myths and Realities About the Estate Tax," Center on Budget and Policy Priorities, August 29, 2013.

the average projected estate tax liability   Liz Pulliam Weston, "5 Estate Tax Myths That Won't Die," *MSN Money*, 2009.

INDEX

243